Why Do They Call It Topeka?

How Places Got Their Names

D0094148

JOHN W. PURSELL

A CITADEL PRESS BOOK
Published by Carol Publishing Group

to Carmelita Pursell

A Citadel Press Book
Published by Carol Publishing Group
Citadel Press is a registered trademark of Carol Communications, Inc.
Editorial Offices: 600 Madison Avenue, New York, N.Y. 10022
Sales and Distribution Offices: 120 Enterprise Avenue, Secaucus, N.J. 07094
In Canada: Canadian Manda Group, One Atlantic Avenue, Suite 105,
    Toronto, Ontario M6K 3E7
Queries regarding rights and permissions should be addressed to Carol
    Publishing Group, 600 Madison Avenue, New York, N.Y. 10022

Carol Publishing Group books are available at special discounts for bulk purchases, sales promotions, fund raising, or educational purposes. Special editions can be created to specifications. For details, contact Special Sales Department, Carol Publishing Group, 120 Enterprise Avenue, Secaucus, N.J. 07094

MANUFACTURED IN THE UNITED STATES OF AMERICA
10 9 8 7 6 5 4 3 2 1

Library of Congress Cataloging-in-Publication Data

Pursell, John W.
    Why do they call it Topeka? : how places got their names / by John
W. Pursell.
        p.   cm.
    "A Citadel Press book."
    ISBN 0-8065-1588-0
    1. Toponymy. I. Title.
G100.5.P87 1994
910'.014—dc20   94-17790
                                                                CIP

Why Do They Call It Topeka?

Contents

Introduction

There is a rich history in every place-name. *Why Do They Call It Topeka?* is a compendium of how places—including U.S. states and cities, as well as nations, cities, waterways, and mountains around the world—got their names.

In the United States, many places were named after the Native American tribes that lived in a particular area. Other places were named after major rivers. Later, when the Europeans began to settle the land, new communities were named after the settlers' hometowns in their country of origin or after leaders in the growing colonies, or even by accident. In other countries, places were named for the landscape or after the inhabitants. No matter what the origins, the stories of where the names came from can be fascinating.

Acknowledgments

The process of compiling a book such as this can only be described as a labor of love. For their labors in assisting me I would like to thank the following individuals: Chak Lai, for his generous assistance with the Chinese entries; Millie Foss, for her vast knowledge of Native American cultures and languages; Jann Fowler-Cornfeld, for her superlative contributions relating to African entries; and to Jim Sellgren, for making available to me a host of resources. Thanks are also due to my literary agent, Joseph S. Ajlouny, and my editor, Bruce Shostak, for their unfailing support. Extra special thanks are owing to Deborah Dwyer and Gwen Foss for their tireless fact-checking, numerous suggestions, and good cheer. As always, in a book that is filled with so many facts, some which are still in doubt, if there are any errors within these pages, the fault is mine and mine alone.

PART *I*

The United States

1

The Fifty States

Alabama was named for the Alabama River, which derives its name from the Choctaw words *alba amo*, meaning "thicket clearers." This term referred to a group of Creek who were farmers. Europeans corrupted the name and called them Alibamu.

These people were among the most adept farmers of North America. Corn was their chief product, and they cultivated it along with beans, pumpkins, and other squash. They also raised flocks of turkeys, some of which numbered in the thousands. When Europeans came to America, the indigenous people were growing thirty-seven varieties of beans. However, their greatest contribution to the world's agriculture was corn, which was developed by crossing certain wild grasses in the region we now call Mexico. Until they were driven out by European settlers in the nineteenth century, these farmers were prosperous, building many fortressed villages and developing a complex and ordered social structure.

Alabama was settled by Europeans in the eighteenth century and became a state in 1819.

Alaska. The name Alaska derives from the Aleut word *alakshak*, meaning "peninsula," "great land," or "mainland." The name applied to the Native people who inhabited the mainland, as opposed to island dwellers.

In 1741, when Danish captain Vitus Bering (1681–1741) arrived in the area exploring for Russia, there were estimated to be seventy-five thousand Aleut and Inuit living there. Russia established the first white settlement there in 1784. Alaska owes its name to Senator Charles Sumner of Massachusetts, whose three-hour speech in 1867 persuaded the Senate to spend about two cents per acre to buy the land from Russia. In his speech, Sumner used the descriptive Aleut word to denote the land mass that was then known as Russian America. After the United States paid Russia $72 million for the acreage, the Aleut term became its new name. Alaska became a state in 1959.

Arizona derives from the Papago words *aleh zon*, meaning "small spring." When Spanish settlers came into the desert to live, each welcome little spring or waterhole was pointed out to them by the Papago as *aleh zon*. The Papago called the land *Aleh-zonac*, meaning "place of small springs." To the Spanish, it became *Arizona*.

Native Americans have lived in this desert region since approximately 10,000 B.C.E. Sophisticated irrigation systems made it possible for them to propagate the dry desert land. These engineering feats were later used by European American settlers who founded the city of Phoenix. Arizona became a state in 1912.

Arkansas derives from the Algonquin word *ugakhpah* or *quawpaw*, meaning "downstream." This name was applied to a southwestern tribe of the Dakota who followed the Mississippi and the Arkansas Rivers. French explorers recorded a Native American village and tribe called Arkansea in 1673. Another spelling was Arkansa, with the plural being Arkansas.

The Europeans named the Arkansas River after the Ugakhpah, and later the state was named for the river. The term *Ozark* is derived from the French descriptive *aux arcs*, pronounced "oh's arks," meaning "in the land of the Arkansas." Arkansas became a state in 1836.

California. The name California first appeared in 1510 in a Spanish romance entitled *Las sergas de esplandian* (The Exploits of Esplandian) by Ordóñez de Montalvo. In the book, California was an imaginary treasure island. Spanish explorers gave the name to Baja California (Lower California, a peninsula in what is now Mexico) and Alta California (Upper California, a large region north of the peninsula). Possible linguistic origins for the name are the Latin *calida forno*, "hot furnace," or the Spanish *calif*, "sovereign."

California, which attained statehood in 1850, is the most populous state in the Union. It has a variety of climates and landscapes that appeal to people. The great majority of newcomers are drawn to California, however, because they believe that California is a land of opportunity, and very few of them have been disappointed.

Colorado got its name from the Spanish word *colorado*, meaning "red" or "reddish," referring to the brownish red color of the Colorado River. Colorado became a state in 1876 and took its name from the river.

Several of our states took their names from rivers, among them: Arkansas, Minnesota, Mississippi, Missouri, Ohio, Oregon, and Tennessee. Rivers were very important in the lives of both Native Americans and early European settlers. Half a dozen of our country's major rivers have their origin in Colorado.

Connecticut. The name Connecticut derives from the Algonquin word *quinnetikq-ut*, which means "at the big tidal river." The name was used by the Mohegan (Mohican) to refer to the Connecticut River, and to Mohegan villages beside it. Later the name was applied to the English colony which was first settled in 1633.

One of the thirteen original colonies, Connecticut became a state when it ratified the Constitution in 1788.

Delaware was named in 1610 for Thomas West, Lord De La Warr (1577–1618), first British governor of the colony of Virginia, by Captain Samuel Argall, a Virginian. Argall gave the name to Delaware Bay, and the colony took its name from the bay. Later the Leni-Lenapé were called the Delaware by European settlers. Strange as it may seem, Lord De La Warr never visited the place that was named for him.

One of the thirteen original colonies, Delaware became the first state when it ratified the Constitution in 1787.

Florida was named on Easter Sunday in 1512 by Spanish explorer Juan Ponce de León (1460–1521). He called it *Pascua Florida*, meaning "Easter." The Spanish name for Easter literally means "feast of flowers," and has been interpreted to mean that Ponce de León was impressed by the many flowers in the area. He landed just north of what is now St. Augustine, and quickly decided he had landed on a island, since three sides of Florida are bounded by water. According to what he had heard, the Fountain of Youth he was seeking was located on an island.

Spaniards began to colonize the area around St. Augustine in 1566, and set up missions to convert the Native Americans to Catholicism. England acquired the territory in 1763, and the United States took possession in 1821. During the period from 1750 to 1835, much of Florida was inhabited by Creek and Seminole, who had settled there after being driven out of Georgia and Alabama. The U.S. government then attempted to remove them to Oklahoma by force, leading to the Seminole War (1835–1842), in which all but three hundred were wiped out. Florida became a state in 1845.

Georgia was named for King George II of England in 1733, when James Oglethorpe, a member of the British Parliament, arrived at what is now Savannah with 120 settlers. The king had granted Oglethorpe a royal charter to the land, and a settlement was founded there as a haven for debtors.

One of the thirteen original colonies, Georgia became a state when it ratified the Constitution in 1788.

Hawaii. Legend has it that the Hawaiian Islands were named after the first Pacific settler, Hawaii Loa, who might have arrived in approximately 400 C.E. Captain James Cook (1728–1779), the first European visitor, named them the Sandwich Islands, after his patron, the Earl of Sandwich. Hawaii is the most recent territory to become a state, joining the Union in 1959.

The Hawaiian Islands were made by volcanoes, one of which is so high that it is covered with snow most of the time. Lake Waiau, near the top of the volcano known as Mauna Kea, is 13,200 feet high, the highest lake in the United States.

Idaho   is believed to have gotten its name from a Shoshone phrase, *Ee-dah-how*, translated loosely as "Look, the sun is coming down the mountain." When the Shoshone saw the first rays of the early morning light on the mountain peaks, it is said, they would greet one another with this phrase. When the territory was established in 1863, the name Idaho was selected. It is a fitting name, indeed. Dawns are startling and beautiful in Idaho. While the valleys are still dark, the snow-clad peaks gleam with the rays of the rising sun, and the growing light moves slowly down the mountains.

However, some believe the name was coined by lobbyist George M. Willing, who merely claimed it was a Native American word, which he translated as "gem of the mountains." Idaho became a state in 1890.

Illinois   takes its name from a confederation of Native American tribes called the Inini, which included the Peoria, Kaskaskia, and Cahokia. *Inini*, meaning "accomplished human beings," was pronounced "Illini" by the French, who called the group the *Illinois*, meaning "Illini people."

In 1673, explorers Jacques Marquette (1637–1675) and Louis Joliet (1645–1700) visited what is now Illinois and claimed it for France. Later, French pioneers built forts at Starved Rock and Peoria. For ninety-two years, Illinois was part of France. Names such as Des Plaines, Champaign, and La Salle reflect the French influence. Illinois became a state in 1818.

Indiana   means "land of the Indians." The Native peoples of America were called Indians by Christopher

Columbus, who mistakenly believed he had sailed to India, and this erroneous name has persisted for five hundred years. Many cities in Indiana have Native American names, among them: Kokomo, Mishawaka, Muncie, Osceola, Pottawattomie Park, Roanoke, Shawnee, Shipshewana, Winamac, and Winona.

Most prominent in Indiana is a name from the Miami language, *Wahba-shik-ki*, which today is the well-known Wabash. The name means "pure white" and refers to a limestone bed in the Wabash River. Indiana became a state in 1816.

Iowa   was named for the Iowa River, which derives its name from *Aiouez,* the French version of the name of a Dakota tribe called the *Ouaouiatonon,* meaning "sleepy ones." This tribal name appears on a 1673 French map, but European explorers soon shortened the name to Ioway or Iowa. The United States came into possession of the territory in 1803 with the Louisiana Purchase, and Iowa became a state in 1846.

Kansas   derives its name from the Kansas River, which was named for the *Kansa,* a Native American group whose name means "south wind people." The Kansa were a southwestern branch of the Dakota and were first met by Spanish explorer Juan de Oñate in 1601. What is now Kansas became U.S. territory in 1803 with the Louisiana Purchase, and Kansas became a state in 1861.

Kentucky   was named for the Kentucky River, which derives its name from the Iroquois word *kentsa,* meaning "level," or the Cherokee phrase *ken-tah-teh,* meaning "land of tomorrow" or "meadowlands."

European exploration of what is now Kentucky began in the seventeenth century, and European settlement was largely made possible through the Cumberland Gap, a natural passage through the formidable Appalachian Mountains. The name Kentucky was first applied to a part of Virginia that was organized as a county in 1776. Kentucky was separated from Virginia and became a state in 1792.

Louisiana was named in 1682 by French explorer Robert Cavelier, sieur de La Salle, in honor of King Louis XIV of France. La Salle and a company of twenty-three Europeans and eighteen Native Americans journeyed south down the Mississippi River. When they found the mouth of the river, they erected a tall wooden post, upon which was carved the name of the king of France and the date, April 9, 1682. La Salle then claimed the land in the name of Louis XIV of France.

French and Spanish settlers populated the southern area of the state, strongly influencing its present culture. Many French colonists from Acadia (eastern Canada) migrated to Louisiana in the 1750s; they were called Acadians, a name which was shortened over time to Cajun. Louisiana was acquired by the United States in 1803 as part of the Louisiana Purchase and became a state in 1812.

Maine was named for the former province of Maine in France. The term also reflects the fact that the mainland was separate from the offshore islands, but this is not the primary source of the name. In the sixteenth century, French explorers called the area east of the Kennebec River Acadie (Acadia, now eastern Maine and part of Canada), and the area to the west was called Maine.

Originally, the province of Maine lay between the Kennebec River and the Merrimac River, which runs through the center of present-day New Hampshire. In 1658, residents of this province agreed to become part of the Massachusetts Bay Colony, and a royal charter in 1691 accomplished this. Maine was split from Massachusetts in 1820, when Congress agreed to admit the slave state Missouri to the Union, in order to maintain an equal number of slave and free states.

Maryland was named for Queen Henrietta Marie (1609–1699), wife of King Charles I of England. Charles granted a charter for Maryland in 1612 and, when asked for a name for the new colony, proposed to honor his wife. The colony's Roman Catholic founders may have also associated the name with the Virgin Mary, but this was only in addition to its primary source.

Maryland is the most unusual of all the states in that at one point between Pennsylvania and Virginia it is little more than a mile wide. This is the narrowest width of any state. The Chesapeake Bay divides the state into an eastern and western shore, thus providing the state with many fine harbors. One of the thirteen original colonies, Maryland became a state when it ratified the Constitution in 1788.

Massachusetts derives from the Algonquin words *massa*, "great," and *wachuset*, "hill," referring to the Blue Hills near Boston. This name was also used to refer to the Massachuset, a Native American tribe that lived in the area of what is now Massachusetts Bay. After European settlers arrived in 1620, the tribe was all but wiped out by a plague.

A royal charter from England established the Massachusetts Bay Colony in 1629. The number of European settlers in the area increased quickly, and lucrative trade was established. British taxation and oppression of the Massachusetts colonists led to the beginning of the Revolutionary War in 1775. Massachusetts became a state when it ratified the Constitution in 1788.

Michigan was named after Lake Michigan, which derives its name from the Fox term *mesikami*, meaning "large lake," or from the Ojibway term *michi-gama*, meaning "great water." These two languages belong to the same language group commonly called Algonquin.

Michigan is the only state comprised of two peninsulas completely separated by water. Georgia is said to be the largest state east of the Mississippi, but if you count its water area, Michigan is the largest. Michigan is called the Great Lakes State because it touches all but one of the Great Lakes. Its two square miles of water for every three square miles of land give Michigan the greatest proportion of fresh water of any state in the world. Until Alaska became a state, Michigan's 3,121 miles of shoreline gave it the longest shoreline of all the states.

European domination of Michigan began mainly with French fur trappers in the 1660s. In 1805, the United States established the Michigan Territory, and in 1837, Michigan became a state.

Minnesota was named for the Minnesota River, which derives its name from the Dakota words *minne*, "water," and *sota*, "sky tinted," or "reflecting cloudy skies." This name was first applied to what is now the Minnesota River, then to the territory occupied by the Dakota. Finally, the name came to be applied to the entire region known as the state of Minnesota. The territory was acquired by the United States in 1803 as part of the Louisiana Purchase and became a state in 1858.

Mississippi was named for the Mississippi River, which derives its name from the Algonquin words *mescha*, "great," and *cebe*, "water." A French record of 1666 showed the name as Messipi.

European settlement of the area began in 1699 with the arrival of French immigrants. In 1798, the U.S. government organized the Mississippi Territory, comprising what is now Mississippi and Alabama. After the Louisiana Purchase in 1803, the Mississippi River basin was added to U.S. territory, and Mississippi became a state in 1817.

Missouri derives its name from a Dakota tribe that called itself *Missouri*, meaning "people with the long canoes." Europeans applied this name to the Missouri River, and later the name was applied to the state.

France claimed the entire Mississippi valley, including what is now Missouri, because of La Salle's travels in 1682. After France suffered defeat in the French and Indian Wars (1754–1763), it secretly ceded to Spain all of its territory west of the Mississippi. In 1800, Napoleon regained possession of the region for France. Three years later, however, Napoleon needed money to fight his war in Europe and sold the Louisiana Territory to the United States for $15 million. Missouri became a state in 1821.

Montana derives from the Spanish or Latin word *montana*, meaning "mountainous." The name was given to the state by James M. Ashley of Ohio, then chair of the House Committee on Territories and later one of Montana's territorial governors. Montana became a state in 1889.

The Rocky Mountains cover the western two-fifths of Montana. These towering mountains form the roof-top of the continent. They might be thought of as the spine of America, which divides the west-flowing rivers, such as the Columbia and the Missouri, from the ones that flow east.

Nebraska derives its name from the Omaha name *Nib-thaska* or *Nibrathka*, meaning "flat water," which referred to the Platt River. The name is related in meaning to the river's present name; *platte* is a French term meaning "flat." The Platte River is very wide and shallow.

What is now Nebraska became a U.S. possession in 1803 with the Louisiana Purchase and was reserved for Native Americans only. In 1854, however, it was opened to settlement, and in 1867, Nebraska became a state.

Nevada derives its name from the Sierra Nevada, a mountain range in the western part of the state. In Spanish, the word *sierra* means "mountains," and *nevada* means "snow clad."

What is now Nevada was once part of Upper California under the jurisdiction of Spain. It then fell under the rule of Mexico in 1821. The United States acquired the region in 1848, and a year later, it became part of the territory of Utah, which Mormon settlers named Deseret. In 1861, the Nevada Territory was officially created, and in 1864, Nevada became a state.

New Hampshire was named after the county of Hampshire, England. Captain John Mason (1586–1635), former governor of Portsmouth, Hampshire, was given a land grant in 1622 for the area between the Merrimack and Piscataqua rivers. He named the land for his home county in England. The New Hampshire town of Portsmouth soon became a thriving port, emulating its namesake.

One of the thirteen original colonies, New Hampshire became a state when it ratified the Constitution in 1788.

New Jersey was named after the island of Jersey in the English Channel. James, duke of York and Albany (later King James II, 1633–1701), received the largest land grant ever given by the English crown, and parceled out what is now New Jersey to two of his favorites, Lord Berkeley and Sir George Carteret. James is believed to have named the colony in honor of Sir George, who was born on Jersey and was its principal royal defender during the English Commonwealth. The island of Jersey is the place where Jersey cattle originated.

One of the thirteen original colonies, New Jersey became a state when it ratified the Constitution in 1787.

New Mexico derives its name from Mexico, which was named for the Aztec war god Maxitel. Spanish conquerors came to the region from Mexico in 1540 to search for the gold of the mythical Seven Cities of Cibola. They found only six small villages where the Hopi and Zuñi lived. They named these people *Pueblo*, a Spanish word meaning "village." This was the first time that horses and cattle were brought into this part of the country.

What is now known as New Mexico was claimed by Spain in the sixteenth century and became a province of Mexico in 1821. The United States acquired it in 1848, after defeating Mexico in the Mexican-American War. New Mexico became a state in 1912.

New York was named for James, duke of York and Albany, who was to become King James II of England. The name York derives from the Anglo-Saxon name *Eorvic*, which means "water dwelling" or "river dwelling." James received a land grant to a large portion of what is now the northeastern United States in 1664, and many New England locales were named for him.

Dutch settlers first claimed the area in 1624 and named it New Netherlands. In 1664, the English conquered the Dutch and renamed the colony New York. One of the thirteen original colonies, New York became a state when it ratified the Constitution in 1788.

North Carolina. The region was named *Carolina*, meaning "land of Charles," in 1562 by French explorer Jean Ribaut, in honor of King Charles IX of France. The name was derived from *Carolus*, the Latin form of Charles. However, this is not the origin of the present name. The British claimed the land in 1629, and in 1663, they named the region Carolina in honor of King Charles I of England. In 1710, Carolina was divided into North Carolina and South Carolina.

One of the thirteen original colonies, North Carolina became a state when it ratified the Constitution in 1789.

North Dakota derives its name from the Dakota, a large Native American group, who are also called Lakota or Nakota. The French named them *Sioux*, meaning "vipers" or "enemies," a name which was not at all liked by the Dakota. The name *Dakota* means "allies," and actually refers to a confederation of several tribes. The name was originally applied to the entire Dakota Territory, and was divided into North Dakota and South Dakota in 1889, when they both became states.

Ohio was named for the Ohio River, which derives its name from the Iroquois term *ohion hiio*, meaning "beautiful river," or possibly from the Wyandot word *ohezuh*, meaning "great" or "fair to look upon." Although the Missouri River is longer, the Ohio is the most commercially important tributary of the Mississippi.

What is now Ohio was inhabited by Native Americans as early as 9,000 B.C.E. In the seventeenth century, the explorer La Salle arrived, establishing a French claim to the region. France sold the territory to the United States as part of the Louisiana Purchase in 1803, and in the same year, Ohio became a state.

Oklahoma derives from the Choctaw words *okla*, "people," and *homa*, "red." The name was suggested in 1866 by the Reverend Allen Wright, a Choctaw chief, to designate what was then known as the Indian Territory. The name was given to a railroad station which later became Oklahoma City.

In 1819, the U.S. government began to remove Native American peoples from the east and drive them to Oklahoma. From 1830 to 1842, thousands of Cherokee, Chickasaw, Choctaw, Creek, and Seminole died of disease, starvation, and mistreatment along the way, and the journey became known as the Trail of Tears.

The Territory of Oklahoma was organized in 1890, and Oklahoma became a state in 1907.

Oregon was named for the Oregon River (now the Columbia River), whose name came from the Shoshone
phrase *oyer-un-gon*, meaning "place of plenty," or possibly from the words *ogwa*, "river," and *pe-on*, "west."
Poet William Cullen Bryant (1794–1878) wrote in his
Thanatopsis, "Where rolls the Oregon, and hears no
sound save its own dashing." The popularity he gave
the name spread the name Oregon over the whole region. The French word *ouragan* means "hurricane,"
but is not thought to be the source of the river's name.

Oregon was first settled by Asian immigrants in approximately 8,000 B.C.E. Europeans visited the area in
the sixteenth to eighteenth centuries but did not lay
claim to the region until 1794, when English captain
George Vancouver (1757–1798) explored the Pacific
northwest coast. Methodist Jason Lee (1803–1845) established a mission in the area of present-day Salem,
leading to large-scale arrival of settlers in wagon trains
from the east. Oregon became a state in 1859.

Pennsylvania was named for Admiral Sir William
Penn (1621–1670), the father of William Penn
(1644–1718), founder of the colony. Charles II of England proposed to name the colony for its founder, but
William Penn was unwilling to be so honored. Being a
Quaker, and believing strongly in the absolute equality
of all people, he was uncomfortable being set above
others. As a compromise, he suggested that the colony
be named in honor of his father, and the king accepted.
Penn established the colony as a refuge for Quakers
and other victims of religious persecution, and Pennsylvania became known as the Quaker State.

The name derives from Penn combined with the
Latin word *silva*, meaning "woods;" the whole meaning "Penn's woods." Penn had first suggested naming

the colony Transylvania ("land beyond the woods"), but this was turned down. One of the thirteen original colonies, Pennsylvania became the second state when it ratified the Constitution in 1787.

The state of **Rhode Island** was named after Rhode Island in Narragansett Bay, which was named in 1524 by Italian explorer Giovanni da Verrazano (c. 1485–c. 1528). It is said that he likened the island to the Greek isle of Rhodes in the Mediterranean. The largest of several islands in the bay, it is today called Aquidneck, its Native American name, and the state is called Rhode Island.

In 1614, Dutch explorer Adriaen Block sailed by the coast of what is now Rhode Island. The first island he encountered he named for himself. Then he saw an island with red clay banks, and he named it *Roodt Eylandt*, meaning "red island." Some believe this to be the origin of the state's name. One of the thirteen original colonies, Rhode Island became a state when it ratified the Constitution in 1790.

South Carolina was named for King Charles I of England (see *North Carolina*). Originally called Carolina, the colony was divided into South Carolina and North Carolina in 1710. One of the thirteen original colonies, South Carolina became a state when it ratified the Constitution in 1788.

South Dakota derives its name from the Dakota, a large Native American group, who are also called Lakota or Nakota (see *North Dakota*). Originally called the Dakota Territory, the region was split into South Dakota and North Dakota in 1889, and both entities became states.

Tennessee is a corruption of the Cherokee name *Tanasi*, the name of their chief village. The exact meaning of the name is unknown, but some believe it means "river with the big bend," referring to the Tennessee River on which the village of Tanasi stood.

Tennessee was at one time part of a large colony called Carolina, which was divided into North Carolina and South Carolina in 1710. Then, in 1796, what is now Tennessee was separated from North Carolina and joined the Union as a state.

Texas derives from the Caddo word *teyshas*, meaning "allies." The term was used by several tribes to indicate their mutual alliances. Spanish explorers in the 1540s took it to be a tribal name, and recorded it as *Tejas*. The term came to be applied to the area north of the Río Grande, and later was officially given to the state.

The flags of six nations have flown over Texas, more than any other state. The Spanish explored the area in 1519, and the French began settlement in 1685. Texas became part of Mexico in 1821. Disagreements with Mexico led the Texans to revolt, and the independent Republic of Texas was established in 1836. Texas joined the United States in 1845, but in 1861 became a member of the Confederate States of America. Texas was readmitted to the Union in 1870.

Utah derives its name from the Utaw, also called Ute, a Native American tribe whose name means "hill dwellers" or "upper people." What is now Utah was claimed by Spain in the eighteenth century and later became part of Mexico. The United States acquired the territory in 1848 at the conclusion of the Mexican-American War.

The first settlers of European ancestry were Mormons, who came to Utah from New York to escape religious persecution in 1847. They named their land Deseret and soon applied for statehood. Several difficulties, including the prejudice of Congress and the question of slavery, prevented Deseret from becoming a state. In 1895, Utah leaders agreed to prohibit church control of the state, and one year later, Utah was admitted to the Union. A Native American name was chosen rather than a Mormon one, indicating the church's willingness to adhere to the agreement.

Vermont derives its name from the French term *vert mont*, meaning "green mountain." French explorer Samuel de Champlain named the mountains east of Lake Champlain Vert Mont in 1612. The name was later shortened to Vermont. The state's common name is the Green Mountain State.

Vermont was settled by New Hampshire natives, who received English land grants in 1764 from the royal governor of New Hampshire. However, the king of England granted the same territory to New York natives, and in 1770, Ethan Allen (1738–1789) organized a militia called the Green Mountain Boys to defend Vermont from the New York encroachers. One of the thirteen original colonies, Vermont became a state when it ratified the Constitution in 1791.

Virginia was named for Queen Elizabeth I of England, who was known as the Virgin Queen because she never married. Originally, the name referred to all the land claimed by the British in North America.

Virginia has been called the Mother of States because Ohio, Indiana, Illinois, Michigan, Wisconsin, and part of Minnesota were carved out of lands that were once part of Virginia. Kentucky and West Virginia are also former parts of the state. Virginia is also called the Mother of Presidents because four of the first five presidents were from the state. One of the original thirteen colonies, Virginia became a state when it ratified the Constitution in 1788.

Washington was named after George Washington (1732–1799), first president of the United States. It is the only state named for a president. At first, the name Columbia was suggested, but the District of Columbia already had this name. Since there was no territory honoring the father of the country, the name Washington was chosen. Washington became a state in 1889.

West Virginia was named after the state of Virginia, from which it broke away at the beginning of the Civil War.

Colonists in western Virginia, separated from the rest of the state by the Allegheny Mountains, were not supported by the government of Virginia. This division caused much unrest in decades following the Revolutionary War. Antislavery people in western Virginia felt that they should be better represented in the proslavery Virginia Assembly. The breach between eastern and western Virginia widened in 1859 when John Brown, in an attempt to establish a refuge for fugitive slaves, seized the government arsenal at Harpers Ferry, in the western part of the state. Differences grew until 1861, when Virginia voted to leave the Union and join the Confederate States of America. Forty western counties then set up a new state, which they named West Virginia, and joined the Union on June 20, 1863.

Wisconsin was named for the Wisconsin River, which derives its name from the Ojibway name *Wees-kon-san* (also spelled *Wishkonsing* or *Wekousing*), meaning "gathering of waters." French explorers in the seventeenth century recorded the name as *Ouisconsin.* The region was appropriately named, since the waters of ten thousand streams and eight thousand lakes "gather" within the borders of what is now Wisconsin.

The United States established the Northwest Territory in 1787, which included present-day Wisconsin. In 1836, the Wisconsin Territory was formed, and included Iowa, Minnesota, and part of Dakota. Wisconsin became a state in 1848.

Wyoming was named for the Wyoming Valley in Pennsylvania, which derives its name from the Leni-Lenapé words *m'cheu-wo-mink* (also spelled *meche-weaming* or *maugh-wau-wa-ma*), meaning "on the great plain." The name was popularized by British poet Thomas Campbell's "Gertrude of Wyoming" (1809), and it appears in many places throughout the nation.

Most of what is now the state of Wyoming became a U.S. possession in 1803 with the Louisiana Purchase. Small portions of Wyoming west of the Rocky Mountains were at one time part of Oregon, independent Texas, and Mexico. Wyoming became a state in 1890.

2

State Capitals, Cities, Towns, and Points of Interest

Abbeville, Louisiana, was named after Abbeville, France.

Ajlune, Washington, was founded in 1914 and named by settler George Ghosn for his home town, Ajlune, Lebanon (now in Jordan). The name derives from that of the Ajlun Mountains in northwest Jordan. In 1960, the town was flooded by the erection of a dam, and the residents reestablished themselves in the town of Mossyrock, a portion of which is now nicknamed Ajlune.

Akron, Ohio, derives from the Greek word *akros*, meaning "summit." Akron is located in Summit County on a ridge that is several hundred feet above sea level.

Alamo, North Dakota, was named for the Alamo, a famous mission in Texas. The name derives from *alamo*, the Spanish word for "cottonwood," which is plentiful in the area of both the North Dakota and the Texas sites.

Albany, New York, ★ was named for James, duke of York and Albany, who later became King James II of England. Albany derives from the Latin word *albus*, meaning "white," which, in the form of Albania, was applied to the ancient kingdom of the Picts in Britain's mountainous north.

Albuquerque, New Mexico, was named for the duke of Alburquerque, who was viceroy of New Spain at the time. The duke spelled his name Alburquerque, as do his descendants, but the New Mexico community dropped an "r" along the way. The city was founded by Governor Valdez in 1706 and named by him. *Alburquerque* is a Latin name meaning "white oak tree."

Alexandria, Virginia, was named in 1748 in honor of John Alexander, who owned most of the land where the city was built. When it was first settled, it was called Belle Haven or Belhaven. *Belle* is French for "beautiful."

Alhambra, California, was named after Alhambra, the famous Moor palace in Granada, Spain. *Alhambra* is an Arabic name meaning "red."

Allentown, Pennsylvania, takes its name from its founder, William Allen, who was a chief justice of Pennsylvania. It was so named in 1762.

Alliance, Nebraska, was named by G. W. Holdrege, who chose the name because it was a single word and came near the beginning of the alphabet. It was also not in use anywhere in the state, a requirement of the U.S. Post Office Department.

Alliance, Ohio,   was known as Freedom until 1850, the time of the completion of two railroads, the Cleveland & Pittsburgh and the Fort Wayne & Chicago. It was named Alliance in the belief that the two railroads would unite their interests there.

Amana, Iowa.   The Amana Society, a German religious group led by Christian Metz, came from New York to build this city in 1855. Their name came from the biblical mountain which King Solomon had called *Amana*, an ancient Hebrew name meaning "remain true."

Amarillo, Texas,   was first called Ragtown, and came into being as a headquarters for buffalo hunters. As the community grew, its name was changed to *Amarillo*, the Spanish word for "yellow," after nearby Amarillo Creek. The creek got its name due to its yellow banks and yellow flowers. The promoter of the town liked the name so much that he had the hotel and all the business houses painted yellow. Today, Amarillo is the metropolis of the panhandle, noted especially for its livestock auctions, said to be the largest in the world.

Anaconda, Montana,   is one of the greatest copper-mining areas in the world. The mine is a great circular pit made by bulldozers. The man who named Anaconda had been reading how, during the Civil War, General Grant encircled Lee like a great anaconda, a giant snake which wraps around its prey and slowly squeezes it to death.

Anchorage, Alaska, was founded in 1914 as headquarters for the Alaska Railroad. It was called Anchorage because supply ships bringing material for the railroad anchored there.

Anderson, South Carolina, was founded in 1826 and named for General Robert Anderson, a hero of the Revolutionary War.

Ann Arbor, Michigan, was named for Ann Allen and Ann Rumsey. In 1824, four settlers moved to what is now Ann Arbor. The two husbands trained a wild grape arbor where they enjoyed sitting and talking, so they named the place Ann's Arbor, after their wives, both named Ann. The name was later shortened to Ann Arbor.

Annapolis, Maryland, ★ was named for Princess Anne, who later became Queen Anne of England.

Antlers, Oklahoma, took its name from the deer antlers that had been hung from a tree by a Native American to mark the location of a spring.

Ashland, Kentucky, settled in 1786, took its name from Ashland, Henry Clay's estate home in Lexington, Kentucky.

Astoria, Oregon, was named for John Jacob Astor (1763–1848), who established a trading post there in 1811. It was the first European settlement west of the Rocky Mountains.

Athens, Georgia, was named in honor of Athens, Greece, which in classical times was a center of culture. The University of Georgia is located there.

Atlanta, Georgia, ★ was named from the word *Atlantic*, found in the name of the Western and Atlantic Railroad, which refers to the Atlantic Ocean. Atlanta was the southeastern terminus of the railroad.

Atlantic City, New Jersey, was named after the Atlantic Ocean.

Augusta, Maine, ★ was named for Pamela Augusta Dearborn, daughter of General Henry Dearborn, who gave his own name to Dearborn, Michigan.

Austin, Texas, ★ was named for Stephen F. Austin (1793–1836), in honor of his leadership in Texas's struggle for independence from Mexico.

Baltimore, Maryland, was named for Cecil Calvert, second baron Baltimore (1605–1675), the proprietor of the colony of Maryland. Baltimore is the name of a barony in Ireland. The Maryland settlement was established in 1729 close to a deep harbor.

Bangor, Maine, a metropolis in eastern Maine, is nicknamed the Queen City. It got its actual name through an odd mistake. The Reverend Seth Noble, an early pastor there, went to Boston to apply for incorporation for the town. While he was waiting, he hummed the old hymn tune "Bangor," which was named for Bangor, Wales. The clerk, filling out the incorporation papers, asked Noble the name of the town. The pastor, misunderstanding him, thought that he had asked for the name of the tune, and replied, "Bangor." And so, the city has been Bangor ever since.

Barnstead, New Hampshire, was settled in 1727 by pioneers from Barnstable, on Cape Cod in Massachusetts, and Hempstead, on Long Island in New York. They combined the names of their two hometowns to create the name Barnstead.

Barre, Vermont, was at first called Wildersburg, but many of the residents thought that name was not cultured enough. They held a town meeting in a local barn in 1793 to decide between the names Holden, a Mr. Thompson's hometown in Massachusetts, and Barre, a Mr. Sherman's hometown in Massachusetts. The vote ended in a tie, and tempers became so hot that the town's name was finally decided by a fistfight.

The fight took place between the two burly men, Thompson and Sherman. They punched and wrestled and thrashed around on the floor of the barn for some time, their neighbors standing around them, each rooting for his champion. Suddenly Thompson fell and failed to rise, whereupon Sherman jumped up and gasped, "There, by God, the name is Barre." And sure enough, the name has been Barre ever since.

Barrow, Alaska, was named in honor of Sir John Barrow (1764–1848), secretary of the British admiralty, who founded the Royal Geographical Society and supported Arctic exploration.

Baton Rouge, Louisiana. ★ On the high banks above the Mississippi River, Native Americans stripped the bark from a cypress tree and painted it red to mark the boundary between the Houma and Bayogoula tribal lands. They called this boundary post *istrouma*, meaning "red stick." The French were unable to pronounce the Native name for the boundary post, so they used the French words *baton rouge*. A French explorer marked its location on his map, and it has been called

Baton Rouge ever since. Red posts were also some-times erected in Native American camps to indicate war.

Battle Creek, Michigan. Two European surveyors and two Native Americans had a fight on the banks of a creek in Michigan in 1824. It was this battle that gave Battle Creek its name.

Beach City, Ohio, was named in 1872 for Henry Beach, an engineer on the Valley Railroad.

Beals, Maine, is located on Great Wass Island, off the coast of Maine about sixty miles from Bangor. It is said to have been named for a remarkable fellow named Manwaring "Barney" Beal. He was six feet seven inches tall and renowned for his great strength. On one occasion, he knocked over a horse when the ani-mal's driver brought it too close. On another occasion, when Barney was fishing in his boat, he was attacked by British sailors. He took away their guns, broke them over his knee, and threw them back into the boat. When the British kept on with the attack, Beal grabbed one sailor by the arm, snapping it like a wishbone. At another time he won a fight with fifteen men in a tavern.

Bellefonte, Pennsylvania. In French, *belle fonte,* means "beautiful fountain." When the famous French visitor Charles-Maurice Talleyrand-Périgord (1754–1838), saw a large spring here, he exclaimed, "What a beautiful fountain," thus giving the place its name.

Berkeley, California, was named for Bishop George Berkeley (1685–1753), a poet, educator, and philoso-pher.

Bethesda, Maryland, is a Hebrew biblical name meaning "house of mercy."

Bethlehem, Pennsylvania, was founded by Moravians under the leadership of Nicholas Ludwig, Count Zinzendorf. The count named it on Christmas Eve, 1741, as he was singing Christmas carols. The carol which inspired him said, "Bethlehem gave us that which makes life rich."

Billings, Montana, was named for Frederick Billings (1823–1890), president of the Northern Pacific Railway. The railroad company wanted to go through the village of Coulson, but the residents of Coulson demanded too much for the land. The railroad then built its own town, which in a few months became a bustling city. Today, Billings is Montana's second largest city.

Birmingham, Alabama, took its name from Birmingham, England's leading industrial city.

Bismarck, North Dakota, ★ was named by officials of the Northern Pacific Railroad for German statesman Otto von Bismarck (1815–1898), in honor of Bismarck's financial aid to the railroad.

Bloomington, Indiana, was thus named by the first settlers in 1815 because they found so many wild roses blooming in the region.

Boise, Idaho, ★ was named after the Boise River, from *les bois*, meaning "the woods," so named by French Canadians when they saw the trees in the vicinity of the present city. Stately old trees still line the streets of Boise.

Booneville, Kentucky, is believed to have been named for Daniel Boone (1734–1820).

Boot Hill Cemetery, Dodge City, Kansas. Boot Hill is a familiar name which echoes across the lands of the Wild West. In the early 1870s, it is said, two cowboys had a gunfight on a high point overlooking Dodge City. The loser died with his boots on and was buried, boots and all, where he fell. This became known as Boot Hill, where those who met a violent death were buried. A dancer, Alice Chambers, is said to have been the last person buried there. Some years ago, the bodies were removed from the original cemetery, and the City Hall took its place. However, to please visitors who come to the city, a re-creation of Boot Hill was arranged by a dentist, Dr. O. H. Simpson.

Boston, Massachusetts, ★ was named by Puritan settlers in 1630 for Boston, England, the former home of many of its residents.

Bowling Green, Kentucky, takes its unusual name from the fact that nineteenth-century lawyers who came to the county courthouse would pass their idle time bowling on the green of Robert Moore's home.

Bozeman, Montana, was named in honor of pioneer trailblazer John M. Bozeman (1835–1867).

Bremerton, Washington, was named for William Bremer, a German real estate pioneer who founded the city.

Bride's Brook, Connecticut. This waterway took its name, according to legend, from something that happened when Governor Winthrop was marrying a couple. The governor had no authority on the west bank, but a couple who wanted to get married could not cross the stream because it was flooded. So the governor stood on one side of the stream and the couple getting married stood on the other, and the ceremony was completed.

Bridgeport, Connecticut, settled in 1639, was named for the first drawbridge over the Poquonock River. Earlier names were Stratfield and New Fairfield.

Bridger, Montana, was named in honor of Jim Bridger, greatest of all the frontier trailblazers. His ability to guide parties where no one else could find the way was legendary. It was said that he could make a map of any region of the Rockies from memory.

Brigham City, Utah, was founded in 1851 and named for its Mormon leader, Brigham Young (1801–1877).

Bristol, Tennessee, was named for Bristol, England. It was built in 1771 as a trading post on the former site of a Native American village, serving western travelers on the Wilderness Road blazed by pioneer Daniel Boone (1734–1820).

Bristol, Virginia, is contiguous with Bristol, Tennessee.

Broken Bow, Nebraska. This unusual town name came into being when a broken Native American bow was found there in the 1880s.

Brooklyn, New York, was named *Breuckelyn* (meaning "broken land") after a town in the Netherlands. The spelling was later changed to Brooklyn.

Bruce, Wisconsin, was incorporated in 1901 and named for Bruce Weyerhaeuser, a member of the prestigious lumber family.

Brunswick, Georgia, was named for King George III, of the royal house of Brunswick, later changed to the royal house of Hanover. It was named by the General Assembly of Georgia in 1771.

Buffalo, New York, derives its name from the French phrase *belle fleuve*, meaning "beautiful river." However, some say the town was named for the Buffalo Creek, which was named for a Native American who lived there. Herds of buffalo were not known in the area.

Bunkie, Louisiana. Colonel A. A. Haas, the founder of the town, once gave his daughter a mechanical monkey that he had bought for her when he made a trip to New Orleans. His daughter, Maccie, could not pronounce *monkey*, so she called the toy Bunkie. Her own nickname then became Bunkie. Later, when the town was officially incorporated in 1885, her father, in a capricious moment, suggested that the town be named Bunkie after his daughter.

Burlington, Vermont, is the largest city in Vermont. Settled in 1773, it was named in honor of the earl of Burlington.

Butte, Montana, took its name from Big Butte, a volcanic cone to the northwest, which is said to be the richest hill on Earth. *Butte* is French for "bluff" or "hill." Butte mines copper and other ores both from giant open pits, which can be fascinating to visitors, and also from standard underground mines, some of which are over a mile deep.

Cairo, Illinois, was named for Cairo, Egypt, because the first settlers thought its delta resembled the Nile delta in Egypt. (See also *Little Egypt, Illinois.*)

Calais, Maine, was named for Calais, France. Settlers may have chosen the name to reflect their hope that Calais, Maine, would also become an important port.

Calienta, Nevada, is a Spanish name meaning "hot." The town is located near hot springs.

Calistoga, California, was named by a Mormon pioneer, Samuel Brannan, who established a spa there in 1859. He believed that the mineral springs and baths would draw as many visitors as the New York spa Saratoga. It is said that the name was created by spoonerism when Brannan bragged, "I'll make this place the Calistoga of Sarafornia."

Cambridge, Massachusetts. Puritans settled Cambridge in 1630 and called it Newe Towne. The present name was adopted in 1638, in honor of the prestigious university town, Cambridge, England, when John Harvard left a bequest for a college on the site. Harvard University is located here.

Camden, New Jersey. In 1611, an English Quaker named William Cooper settled in the area and began operating a ferryboat across the Delaware River. A settlement grew up around the ferry landing and was called Cooper's Ferry. In 1828, Cooper's Ferry was incorporated and changed its name to Camden, in honor of Charles Pratt, first earl of Camden, an English political leader who had been sympathetic to the American colonies.

Camp David, Maryland.   This presidential retreat was founded in 1942 by Franklin Delano Roosevelt, who named it Shangri-La. It was later renamed by President Dwight David Eisenhower, after his grandson David.

Canal Fulton, Ohio,   was first named Milan, but its name was changed to Fulton in honor of Robert Fulton, inventor of the first commercially successful steamboat. Later the name was changed to Canal Fulton.

Cando, North Dakota,   got its name when county commissioners successfully overruled a challenge to their authority. The town was named Cando ("can do") in commemoration of this feat.

Canton, Ohio,   was named by trader Bezaleel Wells, after his friend John O'Donnell's Baltimore estate, Canton. The estate had been named after Canton, China.

Cape Canaveral, Florida,   home of the National Aeronautics and Space Administration's launch center, takes its name from the Spanish word meaning "canebreak."

Carlin, Nevada, was named in honor of Union army officer William P. Carlin.

Carson City, Nevada, ★ was named in honor of Christopher "Kit" Carson (1809–1868), a famous frontier scout.

Carthage, New York, was named for the ancient city of Carthage, on the northern coast of Africa, which was once part of the Roman Empire.

Cedar Rapids, Iowa, was first settled as Rapids City in 1841 and was incorporated under its present name in 1849. The rapids in the Cedar River, named after the Sauk-Fox name *Mosk-wah-wak-wah*, meaning "red cedar," inspired both names.

Charleston, South Carolina, was founded in 1670, and named for King Charles II of England. Its original name was Charles Town.

Charleston, West Virginia. ★ In 1787, Colonel George Clendenin, a Revolutionary War soldier and Virginia state legislator, bought the land where Charleston now stands. He built a fort there to help establish a highway to the West. A town grew up around the fort, which the colonel named Charles Town in honor of his father, Charles Clendenin. In 1818, the city changed its name to Charleston.

Charlotte Amalie, St. Thomas, U.S. Virgin Islands. The capital of the U.S. Virgin Islands, this town was founded by the Danish in 1673 and named for Queen Charlotte of Denmark (1650–1714).

Charlotte, North Carolina, was named for Queen Charlotte, wife of King George III of England. Incorporated in 1768 and settled by Scottish and Irish families from Pennsylvania, it was the first permanent European settlement in the state.

Chattanooga, Tennessee, was first called Ross' Landing after Creek Chief John Ross, who operated a trading post on the site of the city. Chattanooga is surrounded by mountain ranges. The Creek called one of these mountains *Chat-to-noog-gee*, meaning "mountain rising to a point." Chattanooga received its present name when it was incorporated in 1839.

Cheyenne, Wyoming, ★ was named for the Cheyenne. The Dakota word *cheyenne* means "red talkers" or "people of another speech." Greenville Dodge, chief engineer of the Union Pacific Railroad, gave Cheyenne its name in 1867.

Chicago, Illinois, comes from the Algonquin word *checagou*. The word means "skunk cabbage" and refers to the wild onion and garlic plants which were plentiful in the area.

Chillicothe, Ohio, was laid out by Colonel Nathaniel Massie in 1796, at the mouth of Paint Creek, near a Shawnee village. He named it Massie's Town, by popular demand, but later he named it Chillicothe, after the Shawnee village's name, *Chalagawtha*, meaning "village."

Chisholm Trail. This important cattle trail, stretching from Texas to Kansas, was named for Jesse Chisholm

(c. 1806–1868), a wagon guide who marked the route in 1866.

Cincinnati, Ohio, was named for the Society of Cincinnati, an association of officers who served in the Continental Army during the Revolutionary War. The Society of Cincinnati took its name from a fifth century B.C.E. Roman soldier Cincinnatus, whose name meant "having curled hair." Governor St. Clair suggested the name to honor the officers of the Revolutionary War, and the suggestion met with unanimous approval.

Circleville, Ohio, was named because it was laid out in the form of a circle on the site of a Native American mound.

Clarksburg, West Virginia, was named in honor of General George Rogers Clark (1752–1818), a Revolutionary War hero who was called the Savior of the American West. During the war, he was responsible for preventing the British from capturing several important forts in the Northwest Territory, now Illinois and Indiana. Several towns and settlements were later named for him.

Clarksville, Indiana, was the first authorized European settlement in the Northwest Territory. It was laid out in 1784 by George Rogers Clark and named for him.

Clarksville, Tennessee, was named for George Rogers Clark. It has the oldest operating newspaper in the state.

Cleveland, Ohio, was named for General Moses Cleaveland, a surveyor for the Connecticut Land Company. It is thought that an early newspaper typesetter left an "a" out of the name Cleaveland because there wasn't enough space to spell it correctly before the end of the column. The shorter spelling gradually became standard. The city was founded in 1796.

Clifton, Tennessee, incorporated in 1946, was named for the bluffs (tree-covered hills and cliffs) on the river.

Cody, Wyoming, was named for famous western hero William "Buffalo Bill" Cody (1846–1917), who founded the town in 1897.

Coeur d'Alene, Idaho, derives its name from the French translation of the name of a Skitswish tribe, whose name means "heart of awl." These people were renowned for their shrewd ability as traders.

Columbia, South Carolina, ★ was named for Christopher Columbus.

Columbus, Ohio, ★ was named for Christopher Columbus.

Concord, Massachusetts, was named for an agreement reached between Native Americans and European settlers. Concord comes from the Latin word *concordia*, meaning "agreement" or "harmony."

Concord, New Hampshire, ★ was named in 1765 after the peaceful resolution of a boundary dispute.

Coney Island, New York, is a residential neighborhood of Brooklyn, in New York City. It is believed to have derived its name from the Dutch name *Konijn Eiland*, meaning "rabbit island."

Cooperstown, New York, was named for William Cooper, the father of author James Fenimore Cooper. He settled there with his family and surveyed the site in 1785.

Coshocton, Ohio, was named after an Unami village, which got its name from Chief Coshocton of the Unami, also called the turtle clan of the Leni-Lenapé. The name means "finished" or "completed." The village occupied the site of the present city's lower streets, stretching along the riverbank, below the junction of the Tuscarawas and Muskingum rivers. The town was founded by Christian missionaries led by the Reverend David Zeisberger, who preached the first Christian sermon in Ohio in 1776.

Council Grove, Kansas. Native American leaders often held councils here, in a grove of trees, near the place where the Santa Fe Trail later crossed the Neosho River.

Covington, Kentucky, was incorporated in 1815, and named for General Leonard Covington (1768–1813), a hero of the War of 1812.

Crisfield, Maryland, was incorporated in 1872 and named for railroad developer John Crisfield.

Crockett, Texas, was named for Davy Crockett (1786–1836), hero of the Alamo. Crockett is one of the few communities to enjoy its trees as well as make money from them. More than ten thousand pecan trees line the streets, providing shade as well as revenue from nuts.

Cullman, Alabama, took its name from Colonel John Cullman (1823–1895), who was instrumental in bringing large numbers of German settlers to the region. The county, also named in his honor, was founded in 1877.

Cumberland, Maryland, and **Cumberland, Rhode Island**, were named for William Augustus, duke of Cumberland, the son of King George II of England.

Custer, South Dakota, was named for General Armstrong Custer (1839–1876), a career officer who was famous for killing thousands of Native Americans.

Dagsboro, Delaware, was named for Colonel John Dagsworthy, a hero of the French and Indian Wars.

Davenport, Iowa, was named for George Davenport (1785–1845), a fur trader who helped to found the town in 1836.

Dayton, Ohio, was named for Jonathan Dayton (1760–1824), who speculated in land near the site of the present city.

Daytona Beach, Florida, was named for Mathias Day, who founded the city in 1870. The suffixes -*ton* and -*a*, both meaning "place," were added to form this unusual coinage.

Deadwood, South Dakota. In 1875, James Pearson discovered gold in the northern Black Hills in 1875, in a gulch (deep ravine) where there were many dead trees. In just a few months, more than twenty-five thousand people had moved into the area looking for gold. The place became known as Deadwood Gulch. When the town was laid out in 1876, it was named after Deadwood Gulch.

Dearborn, Michigan, was named after General Henry Dearborn (1751–1829), a Revolutionary War hero.

Delmar, Delaware, is located on the border of Maryland. It got its name from a combination of *Del*aware and *Mar*yland.

Denver, Colorado, ★ was named in 1858 for James William Denver, governor of the Kansas Territory, of which Colorado was then a part.

Des Moines, Iowa, ★ was named for the Des Moines River, which got its name from the French phrase *Riviére des Moines*, meaning "river of the Moingwenas." The Moingwenas, a group of Native Americans, became part of the Peoria tribe shortly after 1700.

Detroit, Michigan, lies on the Detroit River, a short strait connecting Lake Erie to Lake St. Clair, a relatively small lake fed by Lake Huron. Founded as a trading post and fort in 1701 by French explorer Antoine de la Mothe Cadillac, he named it *Fort Ponchartrain du Détroit*, "Fort Ponchartrain on the straits." The name was soon shortened.

Donelson, Tennessee, was named for Rachel Donelson Jackson, wife of President Andrew Jackson (1767–1845).

Dover, Delaware, ★ was named by William Penn in 1683 for Dover, England. Dover, located on the Strait of Dover in the English Channel, means "the waters." Towns in Delaware, New Hampshire, New Jersey, and Ohio were also named after Dover, England.

Dubuque, Iowa, was named for Julien Dubuque (1762–1810), a French Canadian who in 1788 negotiated with the Fox to mine lead in the area.

Duluth, Minnesota, was named for French explorer Daniel Graysolon (1649–1710), who took the title sieur du Lhut. Graysolon was one of the first Europeans to touch what is now Minnesota.

East Canton, Ohio, was originally named Osnaburg, possibly after a Native American Chief named Osna. It was later named East Canton because it is east of Canton, Ohio.

Egg Harbor, Wisconsin, got its unusual name when a nest of duck eggs was found at the harbor.

El Paso, Texas. Spanish priests founded a mission here in 1659. The place was named *El Paso*, "the pass," a Spanish phrase which refers either to the ford over the Río Grande or the pass through the Sierra Madre or Franklin Mountains.

Emerson, Nebraska, was named for author and philosopher Ralph Waldo Emerson (1803–1882).

Enderlin, North Dakota, was named in a light moment by settlers who struck out from the terminus of the nearby railroad. The name is a corruption of "end of the line."

Englewood, Tennessee, was first known as Mortimer after its first postmaster. It later became a railroad intersection and was named Tellico Junction. Prominent citizen Nannie Chestnut then named it after Englewood, a village in England, because it reminded her of Robin Hood's home deep in the forest.

Erwin, Tennessee, was named for its first county clerk, Dr. Jessie N. Erwin, who donated land to the community.

Eugene, Oregon, was named for Eugene Skinner (1809–1911), who settled there in the 1840s.

Eureka, Colorado. *Eureka* is a Greek term which means, "I have found it." There are also towns with this name in California, Illinois, Kansas, and Nevada. They may have been named for the discovery of rich natural resources, or just for the acknowledgment that the area would be a good place to settle.

Evanston, Illinois, was named for Dr. John Evans of Attica, Indiana, a founder of Northwestern University, which is located in the city.

Everglades. This 1.5 million-acre Florida swampland is believed to have derived its name from a distortion of the word *river* ("ever") and the southern term *glade*, meaning "marshland."

Fairbanks, Alaska. A gold discovery in 1902 led to the birth of this town. Fairbanks did not grow as rapidly as Nome, because the gold was buried deeper there and required extensive equipment to work. One of the prospectors wrote, "A meeting of the early stampeders was held on newly discovered Pedro Creek, and there was appointed a recorder and we named the place Fairbanks, after the senator who later became vice-president of the United States." Charles W. Fairbanks (1852–1918) was vice president under Theodore Roosevelt.

Fairfield, Connecticut, on Long Island Sound, was named for Fairfield, Kent, England. It was settled in 1639 by Roger Ludlow.

Fall River, Massachusetts, derives its name from a translation of a Native American word which means "falling waters." It is the hometown of Lizzie Borden.

Falls City, Nebraska, was founded in 1857 and named for the falls on the Nemaha River.

Falmouth, Massachusetts, was settled in 1671 and named for Falmouth, England.

Fargo, North Dakota, was named for William G. Fargo (1818–1881) of the famous Wells-Fargo Express.

Fayetteville, Arkansas, was named for the Marquis de Lafayette (1757–1834), a French officer who helped the American cause during the Revolutionary War. **Fayetteville, North Carolina**, and **Fayetteville, Tennessee**, were also named for him.

Findlay, Ohio, was laid out in 1821 and named after Fort Findlay, which got its name from Colonel James Findlay, who built the fort during the War of 1812.

Flagstaff, Arizona. When the United States was one hundred years old, its birthday was celebrated at what is now Flagstaff. A group of travelers made a pine tree into a giant flagstaff and raised an American flag. A settlement grew up around the trimmed tree. The flagstaff stood for many years, and eventually gave the city its name.

Florence, Alabama, was named by an Italian surveyor for Florence, Italy. It was founded in 1818.

Florence, South Carolina, was named for Florence Harllee, whose father was president of the Wilmington and Manchester Railroad.

Florissant, Missouri, was given its name for the French word *florissant*, which means "flourishing" or "prosperous."

Fond du Lac, Wisconsin, derives from the French words *fond du lac*, which mean "the further end of the lake." The city is at the southern end of Lake Winnebago.

Fontana, California, took its name from the Fontana Development Company, which derived its name from the Spanish word *fontana*, which means "fountain."

Forrest City, Arkansas, was named for the Confederate General Nathan Bedford Forrest (1821–1877).

General Forrest took a contract to lay a railroad over Crowley's Ridge, on which the city now stands.

Fort Belvior, Virginia   (military facility), was founded in 1912 and named after the ruins of the Belvior Plantation, owned by Colonel William Fairfax. *Belvior* is a French name which means "beautiful to see."

Fort Benjamin Harrison, Indiana   (military facility), was founded in 1903 and named for Benjamin Harrison (1833–1901), twenty-third president of the United States and veteran of the Civil War.

Fort Bragg, North Carolina   (military facility), was named for General Braxton Bragg (1817–1876), a Confederate officer in the Civil War.

Fort Dix, New Jersey   (military facility), was founded in 1917 and named for Major General John A. Dix (1798–1879), a Civil War officer.

Fort George G. Meade, Maryland   (military facility), was built in 1917 and later named for Major General George Gordon Meade (1815–1872), who commanded the Army of the Potomac during the Civil War.

Fort Gordon, Georgia   (military facility), was founded in 1941 and named for Lieutenant General John B. Gordon (1832–1904), a Confederate Army officer who later became governor of Georgia and a U.S. senator.

Fort Hood, Texas   was founded in 1942 and named for John B. Hood (1831–1879), Civil War commander of the Texas Brigade.

Fort Knox, Kentucky   (military facility), was established in 1918 and named for General Henry Knox (1750–1806), first secretary of war.

Fort Lauderdale, Florida,   was named for Major General William Lauderdale, who built a fort there in 1838. Using the fort as a base, the army searched the Florida Everglades for the Seminole, who were then forcibly removed to the West.

Fort Lee, Virginia,   was built in 1917 and named for General Robert E. Lee (1807–1870), commander of the Confederate Army.

Fort Lewis, Washington   (military facility), was named for explorer Meriwether Lewis (1774–1809) of Lewis and Clark. It is the second largest post in the United States.

Fort McClellan, Alabama   (military facility), was built in 1912 and named for Major General George B. McClellan (1826–1885), a Union commander during the Civil War.

Fort McPherson, Georgia,   was named for Major General James B. McPherson (1828–1864), a Union commander who died during the Battle of Atlanta.

Fort Monroe, Virginia   (military facility), was built in 1819 and named in 1832 in honor of President James Monroe (1758–1831).

Fort Myers, Florida.   The first European settlers came to the site in 1841. They built a fort, commanded by

Colonel Abraham Charles Myers, that was later named in his honor. Later, General Myers was to be the first quartermaster general of the Confederate Army.

Fort Pierce, Florida, was named for Major General Benjamin Kendrick Pierce, a brother of President Franklin Pierce. Two fishing villages, Cantown and Edgartown, were merged and incorporated as the city of Fort Pierce in 1901.

Fort Riley, Kansas (military facility), was built in 1853 and later named for General Bennett Riley (1787–1853), who in 1848 became territorial governor of California.

Fort Shafter, Hawaii (military facility), was established in 1899 and later named for Major General William R. Shafter (1835–1906), who fought in the Civil War.

Fort Sheridan, Illinois (military facility), was built in 1899 and later named for General Philip H. Sheridan (1831–1888), commander in chief of Union forces in 1864.

Fort Wayne, Indiana, was named for General "Mad Anthony" Wayne (1745–1796), a military leader who took the territory from the Native Americans at the Battle of Fallen Timbers in 1794.

Fort Worth, Texas, was named in 1849 for Major General William J. Worth (1794–1849), a hero of the Mexican War.

Foss, Oklahoma, was settled in approximately 1900 and named for J. M. Foss, an early resident.

Fossil, Oregon,   derives its name from the fact that there are so many fossils in the area.

Framingham, Massachusetts,   was settled in 1650 and named for Framingham, England.

Frankfort, Kentucky, ★   was first called Frank's Ford for a pioneer, Stephen Frank, who had been killed by Native Americans at a ford (river crossing) on the Kentucky River. It was later changed to Frankfort.

Freeport, Illinois,   was founded by Pennsylvania Germans in 1850 and named as a protest by Mrs. William Baker, the wife of a trader who freely entertained travelers. She complained that her husband allowed the household to be treated like a "free port" by numerous visitors.

Fresno, California.   The Spanish word *fresno* means "ash tree." Mexican soldiers named the region in the 1830s.

Friendswood, Texas,   was established by Quakers, who refer to themselves as Friends.

Fullerton, California,   was laid out in 1887 and named for George H. Fullerton, an important railroad representative who brought the railroad to the town.

Gabbs, Nevada,   was originally called Toiyabe. In 1943, it was renamed in honor of paleontologist William M. Gabbs.

Gadsen, Alabama,   was founded in 1846 and named for James Gadsen (1788–1858), who negotiated for the

1853 Gadsen Purchase of forty-five thousand square miles of Mexican territory.

Gainesville, Florida,   was founded in 1853 and named for General Edmund Pendleton Gaines (1777–1849), a hero of the War of 1812. **Gainesville, Georgia**, and **Gainesville, Texas**, were also named for him.

Galesburg, Illinois,   was settled in 1836 and named for the Reverend George Washington Gale, a Presbyterian minister.

Galveston, Texas,   was named for the colonial leader of the Spanish possessions along the Gulf of Mexico, Don Bernardo de Galvez. He named it for himself after he occupied the island and drove out the Karankawa, a Native American tribe that was exterminated in 1858.

Garden City, Kansas,   was founded in 1878, and named for the scenic beauty of its many fine gardens. There are Garden Cities in several other states, named for much the same reasons.

Garden of the Gods, Colorado,   (geographical feature). This five-hundred-acre region near Colorado Springs derives its name from the many tall, narrow rock formations which make the place look like the roof of a medieval cathedral covered with spires. In 1859, it is said, it was visited by H. E. Cable and a friend, who said, "This would make a good place for a beer garden." The indignant Mr. Cable retorted, "Beer garden indeed! Why, this is a place fit for the gods to assemble." It has been known as the Garden of the Gods ever since.

Garfield Heights, Ohio. It is thought that this Cleveland suburb got its name from President James Garfield (1831–1881), who walked through the village in the 1850s to attend Hiram College.

Garfield, New Jersey, was named in 1881 for President James Garfield (1831–1881). Earlier names were Cadmus' Melon Patch and East Passaic.

Garland, Texas, was named for U.S. Attorney General Augustus H. Garland (1832–1899).

Gary, Indiana, had its beginning in 1906. It was named for Judge Elbert H. Gary (1846–1927), who was once chairman of the board of directors of the U.S. Steel Corporation, which has a plant there.

Gastonia, North Carolina, was settled near the latter part of the eighteenth century and named for a congressman and judge, William Gaston.

Gatlinburg, Tennessee, was named for Radford Gatlin, who opened a store there in 1855. The local postmaster named the town after Gatlin when Gatlin offered him room in his store for the post office, if he would name the town Gatlinburg.

Georgetown, South Carolina, was named for George, Prince of Wales (1683–1760), who later became King George II of England.

Gettysburg, Pennsylvania, was founded by James Gettys in about 1790 and named for him.

Globe, Arizona, took its name from Globe Mine, which was named for a spherical boulder found there that had markings on its surface looking to some like continents on a globe. It still flourishes as a mining town.

Gnaw Bone, Indiana. Brown County, Indiana, has several communities with unusual names: Needmore, Bean Blossom, and Gnaw Bone. The name Gnaw Bone, it is said, came into being when one man who lived there asked another where a third one was. The second man answered, "I seed him settin' on a log above the sawmill a-gnawin' on a bone." The state tried at one time to get the town's name changed, but was unsuccessful.

Goffstown, New Hampshire, was chartered in 1748 and named for Colonel John Goffe, one of the first settlers.

Golden, Colorado, was established as a mining town, and named for a miner, Thomas L. Golden. Gold and coal are still mined near the city.

Goldsboro, North Carolina, was settled in 1838 and named for Major Matthew T. Goldsborough, of the Wilmington and Weldon Railroad.

Grand Forks, North Dakota, received its name from the fact that the Red River and the Red Lake River unite there. French fur traders who camped there named it *La Grand Fourche*, meaning "the grand forks." Settlers arrived there in 1871. Today, it is the second largest city in North Dakota.

Grand Island, Nebraska. The town's name came from an island in the Platte River called *La Grande Isle*,

French for "the big island." The town was laid out in 1866.

Grand Junction, Colorado, was so named because the Colorado and Gunnison rivers unite there.

Grand Rapids, Michigan, lies on the Grand River, thirty miles east of Lake Michigan. It was named for the river.

Granite City, Illinois, was founded in 1891 as a place where graniteware (enameled ironware) could be made. Some years later, the granite manufacturers, who had come from St. Louis to make their fortunes, went out of business, but the name remained.

Great Falls, Montana, lies near the falls of the Missouri River and derives its name from that fact.

Greeley, Colorado, founded in 1870, was named for Horace Greeley (1811–1872), a prominent journalist who helped to found the first settlement.

Green Bay, Wisconsin. A trading post was established in the vicinity of Green Bay in 1634. In 1669, a Jesuit mission was established, and the settlement was called *La Baie Verte*, French for "the green bay." The name derives from the bay, surrounded by many lush green trees. Later, British traders translated the name and called it Green Bay.

Green River, Wyoming, got its name from the Green River on which it is located. The river derives its name from its deep green color.

Greensburg, Pennsylvania, was named for General Nathanael Greene (1742–1786), a Revolutionary War leader who served as second-in-command under Washington. **Greenville, Mississippi**; Greenville, Ohio; and **Greenville, South Carolina**, were also named for Nathanael Greene.

Greenwich, Connecticut, was named in 1640 for Greenwich, England.

Grindstone River, Minnesota, was so named because, at the time, it held a near monopoly on the making of grindstones. These large circular stones, fitted into the machinery of a mill, provided the grinding action necessary for the creation of flour and other staple items on the frontier.

Groton, Massachusetts, was named for Groton, England, the birthplace of John Winthrop, an early governor of Connecticut.

Gruetli-Laager, Tennessee, was settled around 1869 by Swiss immigrants. This town is formed from two communities, Gruetli and Laager. Gruetli was named for Gruetli, a Swiss canton (province).

Gulfport, Mississippi, was so named because it is a port on the Gulf of Mexico.

Hackensack, New Jersey, was named for the Ackinchesacky, a Native American tribe that lived in the area. The name Ackinchesacky, whose meaning is unknown, was distorted by Europeans, who called them Ackenack, which was further distorted to become

Hackensack. When the Dutch first settled the area in 1713, they called it New Barbados.

Hagerstown, Maryland, was named for its founder, Captain Jonathan Hagar (1714–1775). When he laid out the settlement, he called it Elizabethtown, in honor of his wife, but when it was incorporated in 1814, it was renamed Hagerstown.

Hamden, Connecticut, was settled in 1664, and named for English member of parliament John Hampden.

Hamilton, Ohio, was named for Alexander Hamilton (1757–1804). One of the founders of the United States, he served as the first secretary of the treasury and helped to establish a strong, financially sound government after the Revolutionary War.

Hammond, Indiana, was founded in 1869 and named for George Hammond (1838–1886), a pioneer in shipping refrigerated beef, whose meat-packing plant was the first industry in Hammond. Hammond packed his meat with ice from the nearby river and inland lakes, and also originated refrigerated freight cars.

Hampton, Virginia, was named after Hampton Creek, earlier called Southhampton River, which was named for Henry Wriothesley (pronounced "RIZZ-lee," 1573–1624), third earl of Southhampton. The town grew up around Fort Algernourne, now called Fort Monroe, which was built to protect the James River Canal.

Hamtramck, Michigan, was named for Colonel John F. Hamtramck, the first American commander at Detroit. This city, incorporated in 1798, is now completely surrounded by Detroit. It is the former home of the original Dodge automobile plant.

Harlingen, Texas, was named for Harlingen, the Netherlands, by settler Len C. Hill. Both cities are on barge canals.

Harmony, Pennsylvania, was named for the Harmony Society, a celibate religious group led by George Rapp, who settled here in 1814 after coming from Germany.

Harpers Ferry, West Virginia. Robert Harper was so impressed with the beauty of the area that in 1734 he built a cabin there and established a ferry across the confluence of the Shenandoah and Potomac rivers. The village of Shenandoah Falls grew up around the ferry. The city was later named Harpers Ferry in honor of its first settler. Harpers Ferry was made famous by John Brown's raid in 1859, a critical event preceding the Civil War.

Harriman, Tennessee, was named for Union General Walter Harriman of New Hampshire. In 1864, while moving his army from Mississippi to Knoxville, he camped on the spot where the town now stands. Noting the water supply, the river, the railroad, and the coal and iron deposits, the general remarked that it was an "ideal spot for an industrial development." His son, Walter, came to what is now Harriman, laid out the town, and named it for his father. The Women's Christian Temperance Union, largely responsible for the passage of Prohibition (1919–1933), had its headquarters there.

Harrisburg, Pennsylvania. ★ In 1710, John Harris started a ferryboat service across the swiftly flowing Susquehanna River. The settlement that grew up there became known as Harris' Ferry. Harris and his son, John Harris, Jr., operated the ferry for many years. At one time, the town's name was changed to Louisburg, in honor of King Louis XVI of France, but by 1791, it was renamed Harrisburg in honor of John Harris, Jr., who had laid out the town. It became the state capital in 1812.

Harrodsburg, Kentucky, was named for an early pioneer, James Harrod (1742–1792), who founded the town. Harrodsburg is the oldest European settlement in Kentucky.

Hartford, Connecticut, ★ was named in 1636 after Hertford, England. The English pronunciation of Hertford accounts for the altered spelling of the American name. Today it is known as the Insurance Capital of the World.

Hattiesburg, Mississippi, was named for Hattie Hardy, whose husband was a railroad official who chose the site for the city in 1881.

Haverhill, Massachusetts, was founded in 1640 by the Reverend John Ward, and named for Haverhill, England.

Hayward, California, was originally a Native American campsite. It was named for William Hayward, postmaster, hotel owner, and disappointed gold seeker, who arrived there in 1851.

Hazelton, Pennsylvania, was named for Hazel Creek, which derives its name from the many hazel trees found in the area. It became populated because of its rich anthracite coal. The town was laid out in 1836 by the Hazelton Coal Company.

Helena, Montana, ★ was named by John Somerville, who came from Helena, Minnesota. The town sprang up in about 1864 when gold was discovered in Last Chance Gulch.

Hempstead, New York, was named for Hempstead, the Netherlands. The area was purchased from Native Americans in 1643, and a settlement was established.

Hershey, Pennsylvania, was named for Milton S. Hershey (1857–1945). Hershey founded the town in 1903 as a chocolate manufacturing center. It is still the home of the Hershey Chocolate Corporation.

Hialeah, Florida, took its name from the Seminole words *haiyakpo hili*, which mean "pretty prairie." It was settled in 1910.

High Point, North Carolina, took its name from the fact that it was the highest point on the North Carolina Railroad between Goldboro and Charlotte. It was laid out in 1853.

Highland Park, Michigan, took its name from a local ridge that has now been leveled. It was settled in the 1800s, and was first known as Nabors, then Whitwood. Highland Park is completely surrounded by the city of Detroit.

Hilo, Hawaii, is the second largest city in Hawaii, after Honolulu. The city is situated on Hilo Bay, from which it got its name. The Hawaiian word *hilo* means "new moon."

Hobbs, New Mexico, was named for one of its first settlers, a woman known as Grandma Hobbs, who arrived in 1907.

Hoboken, New Jersey. Early Dutch settlers purchasd the land in the area from the Leni-Lenapé (Delaware), who called the territory *Hobocan Hackingh*, meaning "land of the tobacco pipe." However, some believe the town was named after Hoboken, a Belgian town near the Dutch border.

Holland, Michigan, was named in 1847 by Dutch settlers for their native land.

Hollywood, California, had its beginning in 1853, when an adobe house was built on the site where Los Angeles now stands. Mrs. H. H. Wilcox, in 1887, named it after the home of a friend in Chicago. *Hollywood* means nothing more than "grove of holly."

Hollywood, Florida, was named for Hollywood, California, by its developer, who had lived in California.

Holyoke, Massachusetts, was named either for the Reverend Edward Holyoke, a president of Harvard, or for Eliezur Holyoke, an early explorer in the region.

Honolulu, Hawaii, ★ is from *hono lulu*, a Hawaiian name meaning "sheltered bay."

Hopkinsville, Kentucky, was first known as Elizabethtown. It was later renamed in honor of General Samuel Hopkins (1756–1819), a hero of the War of 1812.

Hot Springs, Arkansas, was known to the Native Americans there as *Minnekahta*, which means "hot water." A trapper, Manuel Prudhomme, founded the first permanent European settlement there in 1874. It took the name Hot Springs when it became the county seat in 1882. Many people journey to Hot Springs to bathe in its mineral waters, which are said to have some beneficial effects on the body.

Houghton, Michigan, was named for Michigan's great geologist, Dr. Douglas Houghton (1809–1845). The area is known for its important copper deposits, which are still being worked there.

Houston, Texas, is the largest industrial city in the southwestern states. It was named for general Sam Houston (1793–1863), who led the army that won Texas independence from Mexico in 1836. It is one of the largest cities in the United States.

Huachuca City, Arizona, derives its name from the Huachuca Mountains, which got their name from the Apache word for "thunder."

Humboltd, Nebraska, was named by the founder in honor of German scientist Alexander von Humboldt (1769–1859).

Huntington, West Virginia, is the second largest city in the state. It was established in 1871 as the terminus of the Chesapeake and Ohio Railroad. The city took its name from Collins P. Huntington, president of the railroad at that time.

Huntsville, Alabama, was named for John Hunt, a Revolutionary War veteran from Virginia, who settled there in 1805. At first it was called Hunt's Spring. Leroy Pope later named the town Twickenham, after the English hometown of his illustrious relative, Alexander Pope. However, it was soon renamed Huntsville.

Huntsville, Texas, was founded as a trading post in 1830 by Pleasant Gray, and named for his hometown in Alabama.

Hutchinson, Kansas, was named for its founder, Indian agent C. C. Hutchinson, in 1872.

Independence, Missouri, settled in 1817, is the seat of Jackson County, which was named for President Andrew Jackson (1767–1845). It was named for Jackson's love of independence.

Indianapolis, Indiana, ★ the largest city in the state, was named after the state of Indiana. *Polis* is a Greek suffix meaning "city."

Inglewood, California, was named after its founder's hometown, Inglewood, Canada.

Ironwood, Michigan. One of the first leaders in iron mining in the state of Michigan was James Wood. He became known as Iron since he mined iron, and this nickname, added to his own surname, gave the city of Ironwood its name.

Irvington, New Jersey, was named for author Washington Irving (1783–1859), whose estate was at nearby Tarryton. At first it was called Capetown, but in 1852, the name was changed to Irvington.

Ithaca, New York, was named after Ithaca, the legendary home of Ulysees. *Ithaca* is an ancient Greek name meaning either "the strait" or "steep." The town was founded in 1879 by General Simeon DeWitt.

Jackson, Mississippi, ★ was named for President Andrew Jackson (1767–1845). **Jackson, Tennessee, Jacksonville, Florida, Jacksonville, Illinois,** and **Jackson, Michigan** were also named for Andrew Jackson.

Jamestown, New York, and **Jamestown, Tennessee** were named for Jamestown, Virginia.

Jamestown, Rhode Island, was named for King James II of England (1633–1701). It was settled in 1672.

Jamestown, Virginia (extinct town), was named for King James I of England (1566–1625). This was the first successful permanent English settlement in the New World, founded in 1607. It was first called James Town. Because Jamestown is not now inhabited, Norfolk, Virginia, claims to be the oldest continuously inhabited European settlement in the New World.

Janesville, Wisconsin, was named for its first postmaster, Henry Janes. It was settled in 1835.

Jefferson City, Missouri, ★ was laid out by Daniel M. Boone, son of Daniel Boone, and named in honor of President Thomas Jefferson (1743–1826).

Jefferson City, Tennessee, was named for President Thomas Jefferson.

Jerome, Arizona, was named for one of the founders, Eugene Jerome, who was a distant cousin of Winston Churchill.

Jerome, Idaho, was named for Jerome Hill, who was a prominent figure in the irrigation project of 1905. His son-in-law or grandson, both also named Jerome, may actually be the source of the town's name.

Jersey City, New Jersey, was named for the state of New Jersey.

Johnson City, New York, was named for the industrialist and philanthropist George F. Johnson. It was first called Lestershire, and took its present name in 1910.

Johnson City, Tennessee, was settled after the East Tennessee and Virginia Railroad was built through the area. A town grew up around the water tank, after which Henry Johnson (1809–1874) built a depot in 1834. The city was first known as Johnson's Depot, but during the Civil War it was called Haynesville, for Landon C. Haynes, a Confederate state senator. It was renamed Johnson City in 1869.

Johnson City, Texas, was founded in 1879 by James Johnson, the uncle of Lyndon B. Johnson, and named for him.

Johnstown, New York, was named for Sir William Johnson (1715–1774), who in the eighteenth century was superintendent of Indian affairs for the British Crown Colony. The suffix *-son* on Johnson's name was replaced with the suffix *-town* to make the name.

Johnstown, Pennsylvania, was founded by a Swiss immigrant, Joseph Johns, in 1793. At first, it was called Conemaugh, but was later named for him. The city was destroyed by a flood in 1889, and rebuilt.

Joliet, Illinois, was originally named Juliet, but in 1845, the name was changed to honor French explorer Louis Joliet (or Jolliet, c. 1645–c. 1700).

Juneau, Alaska, ★ was named for Joseph Juneau, one of the prospectors who found gold in the area in 1880. For many years, gold mining was Juneau's chief activity. However, the wide gap between labor costs and the price of gold idled mining operations after World War II.

Kalamazoo, Michigan, on the Kalamazoo River, got its name from the Algonquin word *kee-ka-la-ma-zoo*, which means either "smoke," "beautiful water," "boiling water," or "otters." It was first called Bronson, after a settler who built a cabin there in 1829, but was renamed Kalamazoo in 1836.

Kankakee, Illinois, on the Kankakee River, got its name from the Mohegan word *kankakee*, which means either "wonderful land" or "wolf."

Kaysville, Utah, was incorporated in 1868 and named for William Kay, the district's first Mormon bishop.

Kearney, Nebraska,　was named for General Stephen W. Kearney (1794–1848), a veteran of the War of 1812 and the Mexican War.

Kearney, New Jersey,　was settled by Scottish immigrants in 1668. Native Americans originally called this area Michgecticok, but it was renamed in honor of Major General Philip Kearney.

Kenosha, Wisconsin,　derives from the Potawatomi word *kenosha*, meaning "pike" or "pickerel." It was first called Pike Creek, due to the abundance of pike, then later, Southport. It took its present name in 1850.

Keokuk, Iowa,　was named for Keokuk (1780–1848), a Sauk chief. His original name was *Kiyokaga*, meaning "he who moves around alert." Settlement of this area began in 1820.

Ketchikan, Alaska,　originated as a fish saltery. It derives its name from the Tlingit words *kach kama*, which mean "eagle wing river." This term applied to the eagle-wing appearance of water flowing over an unusual rock formation in Ketchikan Creek.

Kettering, Ohio,　was named in honor of the industrial scientist Charles Franklin Kettering (1876–1958). The town, organized in 1841 and originally called Van Buren Township, took its present name in 1952. In its early days it was noted for its stone quarries.

Key West, Florida,　derives its name from the Spanish words *cayo hueso*, meaning "isle of bones." The many bones found there by early Spanish explorers were thought to be those of Native Americans killed in battle. However, some assert that the name Key West is merely descriptive of the local geography, *key* meaning "island."

Kingsport, Tennessee, was settled in 1750 around Fort Robinson, on the Old Wilderness Road, a pioneer road to the West. It became a boat landing, and the site was variously called Island Flats, Boat Yard, and Christianville, until 1774, when Colonel James King established a mill on the Holston River at the mouth of Ready Creek. The place then became known as King's Mill Station, and later, King's Port.

Kingston, New York, was founded as a fur trading post in 1610 and called Esopus. In 1661, Dutch pioneer Peter Stuyvesant (1610–1672) renamed it Wiltwyck. When the British gained control of the area in 1664, they named it Kingston, either after Kingston, England, or in honor of King Charles II.

Kingston, Tennessee, was named for Major Roger King, a Revolutionary War officer and early settler.

Kirkwood, Missouri, started as a stagecoach stop and was settled in 1814 by Jesuits. The Pacific Railroad laid a track through the town in 1851, and the place was renamed in honor of chief engineer James Kirkwood.

Knoxville, Tennessee, was first called White's Fort, because Captain James White, a Revolutionary War veteran, built a fort there in 1785, after a treaty with the Cherokee opened the door to settlers. It was renamed Knoxville in 1791, in honor of General Henry

Knox (1750–1806), minister of war in George Washington's cabinet. Settlers chose to honor Knox because they foresaw the need for the army to defend their settlement, and believed the army would support a town named for the minister of war. Although Nashville is the state capital today, on three different occasions, Knoxville served as the capital of Tennessee, for a total of seventeen years.

Kokomo, Indiana, was laid out in 1844 by David Foster, a trader among the Miami. It was named in honor of Kokomo, a Miami chief, whose name means "black walnuts."

Kooskia, Idaho. The name is believed to derive from a Native American name meaning "joining of waters."

La Crosse, Wisconsin, situated on the Mississippi River in the southwestern part of the state, developed around a trading post that was built in 1841. It derives its name from the Native American game *baggataway*, which early French explorers had called *la crosse*. The sticks used in the game resembled the croziers used by French shepherds in a similar game, and so they called the game *la crosse*, "the crozier."

La Habra, California, derives its name from the Spanish word *abra*, meaning "fissure," which refers to an opening in the nearby Puente Hills.

La Porte, Indiana, was settled in 1830 and named *La Porte*, which in French means "the door," due to a natural opening in the forest which served as a gateway to the North.

Lafayette, Indiana, was named in 1825 for Marie Joseph du Motier, marquis de Lafayette (1757–1834), who helped the American colonies gain their independence from England during the Revolutionary War.

Lafayette, Louisiana, was settled by Acadians from Nova Scotia in the latter part of the eighteenth century and called Vermillionville. It was renamed in 1884 in honor of the marquis de Lafayette.

Lakewood, New Jersey, derives from the fact that it is located in a pine forest in a lake region.

Lakewood, Ohio, was named in 1889 for its wooded shore on Lake Erie. It had earlier been known as Rockport (1819) and East Rockport (1871).

Lancaster, California, was named in 1882 for the Pennsylvania home of its founder, M. L. Wicks.

Lancaster, Ohio, was named for Lancaster, Pennsylvania. It was settled by Ebenezer Zane in 1800.

Lancaster, Pennsylvania, was named for Lancaster, a shire (county) in England.

Lancaster, South Carolina, was settled by pioneers from Lancaster, Pennsylvania, who named it for their hometown.

Langtry, Texas, was named by prominent resident Judge Roy Bean in honor of his favorite actress, Lillie Langtry (1853–1929). Once, on a cross-country rail trip, the famed actress had the conductor hold the train until she could visit the town bearing her name. She is buried in Del Rio, Texas, about sixty miles from Langtry.

Lansing, Michigan, ★ was named in 1848 for Lansing, New York, a village from which some of the first settlers came.

Lansing, New York, was named for jurist John Lansing.

Laramie, Wyoming, was founded on the banks of the Laramie River, which in turn got its name from Jacques La Ramie, a French Canadian trapper.

Laredo, Texas, was established in 1755 and named for Laredo, Spain.

Largo, Florida, was settled in 1866 and named for nearby Lake Largo, which in Spanish means "big." The lake has since been drained.

Las Cruses, New Mexico, founded in 1859, derives its name from the Spanish phrase *las cruces,* meaning "the crosses." Some earlier pioneers were massacred at the site, and a later caravan discovered the bodies and buried them, placing wooden crosses at the head of each grave. Travelers applied the name Las Cruses to the area.

Las Vegas, Nevada, derives from the Spanish phrase *las vegas,* meaning "the fertile plains." It was named by Mormon settlers who, in 1855, found artesian springs in a fertile valley.

Laurel, Delaware, was named for the laurel shrubs that are native to the region.

Laurel, Mississippi, was named for the many laurel shrubs found in the area.

Lawrence, Kansas, was founded in 1854 and named for Amos A. Lawrence, a New England textile manufacturer and promoter of the town.

Lawrence, Massachusetts, was named for founder Lawrence Abbot (1792–1855).

Lead, South Dakota. In April 1876, Fred Manuel and his brother Moses made a strike in Gold Rush Gulch. Fred said to his brother, "This is like that home stake you were looking for so long." He was right. Later, George Hearst, one of the world's best-known mining personalities, became interested in the Manuels' discovery. Hearst was a very rich man. With his backing, Homestake Company was soon organized and began its very successful operation. Lead, pronounced *leed*, took its name from the term meaning "lode" or "vein." Lead has the largest gold mine in the United States, Homestake Mine.

Leadville, Colorado, got its name because of the large quantities of silver-bearing lead ore in the area. Copper, iron, and gold are also mined there. The largest molybdenum mine in the world is thirteen miles east of the city.

Leavenworth, Kansas, on the Santa Fe Trail, was named for Fort Leavenworth, which was built in 1827 by General Henry F. Leavenworth (1783–1834). It was the first incorporated town in the Kansas Territory.

Lebanon, Connecticut, was settled in 1695 and named for the biblical Lebanon.

Lebanon, Missouri, was founded in 1849 and named for Lebanon, Tennessee.

Lebanon, Tennessee, was established in 1802 and named for the biblical Lebanon. The many cedar trees in the area reminded settlers of Lebanon's cedars.

Leesburg, Florida, was named for the founders, Calvin and Evander Lee, who settled the area in the 1800s.

Left Hand Canyon, Colorado (geographical feature), northeast of Boulder, was named for Left Hand, an Arapaho chief whose camp was on the site.

Lenoir City, North Carolina, was founded in 1841 and was first known as Tucker's Barn. It was later named in honor of General William Lenior (1751–1839), a Revolutionary War soldier.

Lenox, Massachusetts, was settled about 1750 and named for Charles Lennox, duke of Richmond (1735–1806).

Lesage, West Virginia, was founded when Jules Lesage's steamboat wheel shaft broke. It is said that he got so impatient with the delay that he got off the boat, bought the land, built a house, and started a settlement.

Levittown, New York, is located on Long Island. It grew out of a housing project started in 1946 for veterans of World War II. William Levitt, whose company, Levitt and Sons, built hundreds of cheap houses on former potato fields, named the massive subdivision after himself. He also built Levittowns in New Jersey and Pennsylvania.

Lewistown, Idaho, was named for Meriwether Lewis (1774–1809), who, along with his fellow explorer William Clark, camped near its present site in 1805.

Lewistown, Montana, was named for Major William H. Lewis, who built a fort there in 1876.

Lewistown, Pennsylvania, was laid out in 1790 and named for William Lewis, an early iron manufacturer.

Lexington, Kentucky. One day in 1775, when Simon Kenton was hunting, four surveyors approached him. Simon asked, "Where are you going?" They replied, "To build a station on the Kentucky River." Simon went with the men to show them the way. Captain Robert Patterson was the chief surveyor. When they stopped to camp, a man named Thomas Williams came along the way and excitedly told them that we were at war with England. "They attacked us at Lexington, Massachusetts, on the nineteenth of April, and we whipped 'em good," he said. All the men were thrilled. "This spot," Patterson said as they sat around the campfire that night, "is one of the most beautiful places I've ever seen. One of these days I'm going to come back here and lay out a town, and do you know what I am going to call it? I am going to call it Lexington, in honor of the victory about which we have just heard."

Lexington, Massachusetts, was named for Laxton, England. It became famous as the site of the first battle in the Revolutionary War, and many patriotic settlers adopted the name for their new towns.

Lima, Ohio, was laid out in 1831 and named for Lima, Peru. During the pioneer days, many Ohio settlers had malaria. To treat the illness, they needed quinine, which they got from Peru. In appreciation, they named their community Lima, a name which was drawn from a hat.

Lincoln, Illinois, is the only town named for President Abraham Lincoln (1809–1865) while he was living. The city is near Salem, Illinois, where Lincoln once lived, and also near Springfield, Illinois, where he was practicing law at the time. The town was laid out in 1853.

When Lincoln was told they were planning to name the town for him, he protested, saying, "I never knew anything named Lincoln that amounted to anything." He finally agreed, however, and after the town site had been laid out, a crowd gathered to dedicate it, with Abraham Lincoln as master of ceremonies.

Lincoln took a large watermelon in his hand, which he cut open with his pocketknife and split in two on the wagon on which he was standing. Taking out the core, he squeezed the juice into a tin cup. "I now christen this town site. Its name is Lincoln!" he proclaimed, and poured the watermelon juice on the ground in humorous dedication.

Then Lincoln continued. "I have also prepared a feast for this occasion." He pulled the cover off a load of watermelons, and the crowd did have a feast.

Lincoln, Nebraska, ★ was laid out in 1859, and first called Lancaster, but was renamed for Abraham Lincoln in 1867.

Lincoln, Rhode Island, was named also for Abraham Lincoln.

Little Egypt, Illinois. The nickname Little Egypt is applied to the southern tip of the state, where a large area of fertile land lies at the junction of the Ohio and Mississippi rivers. Settlers believed the rivers to be as important to the region's agriculture as the Nile was to the prosperity of ancient Egypt. (See also *Cairo, Illinois.*)

Little Rock, Arkansas. ★ In 1721, French travelers explored a section of the Louisiana Territory along the Arkansas River, establishing trade with the Native Americans and searching for legendary treasure. For a long time, the Native Americans had spoken of a "green rock" that was upstream at the "point of rocks" along the river. When the French heard about this green rock, they thought it could only mean emeralds, which is why the expedition began.

The explorers found the point of rocks, which they called Grand Rock. Farther down the stream on the south bank, they found a smaller rock, which they named Little Rock. About a hundred years later, a permanent settlement grew up at Little Rock.

Livingston, Tennessee, was incorporated in 1835 and named for Edward Livingston (1764–1836), minister of state in Andrew Jackson's cabinet.

Lockport, New York, was founded in 1821 and grew up around locks on the New York State Barge Canal.

Long Beach, California, was laid out in 1881, and named by the Long Beach Land and Water Company in 1887. The company took its name from the nearby beach, which is eight and a half miles long.

Long Branch, New Jersey, was named for its location on the long branch of the South Shrewsbury River. The land on which it was settled was purchased from the Leni-Lenapé.

Loraine, Ohio, was settled in 1787 by Nathan Perry and named for the province of Lorraine, France.

Los Angeles, California. Spanish missionaries founded Los Angeles in 1781. They named it *El Pueblo de la Reina Nuestra Señora de Los Angeles de Porciuncula*, meaning "the town of the Queen Our Lady of the Angels of the Porciuncula." Porciuncula is a chapel in Assisi, Italy, that was the cradle of the Franciscan order. Most of the name was dropped when the city was incorporated in 1850. Los Angeles is often called by its English equivalent, City of Angels.

Louisville, Georgia, was laid out in 1786 and named for King Louis XVI of France (1754–1793).

Louisville, Kentucky, was laid out in 1773 by George Rogers Clark (1752–1818). It was settled six years later and named after King Louis XVI of France, in honor of France's aid to the American colonies during the Revolutionary War.

Louisville, Mississippi, was named after Colonel Louis Winston, an early settler, or possibly for Louisville, Kentucky.

Louisville, Ohio, was originally named Lewisville after Lewis, one of the twenty-five children of Henry Loutzenheiser, a Pennsylvania German. But since there was already one Lewisville in Ohio, it was later changed to Louisville, which was believed proper.

Lovington, New Mexico, was founded in 1908 on the homestead of R. F. Love and named for him.

Lowell, Massachusetts, was settled in 1653 and later named for textile industrialist Francis Cabot Lowell (1775–1817).

Lubbock, Texas, was named for Colonel Thomas S. Lubbock, one of the signers of the Texas Declaration of Independence. It was settled by Quakers in the 1870s.

Ludington, Michigan, was named for its founder, James Ludington.

Lynchburg, Virginia, was named for John Lynch, a ferryboat operator, who owned the land where the town was built. It was settled by Quakers in 1786.

Lynn, Massachusetts, was named for Lynn Regis (Keltic *lynn*, "pool," and Latin *regis*, "king's"), a locale in England. When it was settled in 1631, it was known as Saugus, but its name was changed to Lynn in 1637.

Macon, Georgia, was named for Nathaniel Macon, a North Carolina congressman. The town developed around Fort Hawkins, and in 1806, it was known as Newton. Its name was changed in 1823.

Madawaska, Maine, was named for Madawaska River, which took its name from the Micmac term meaning "having reeds at the outlet."

Madison, Wisconsin, ★ was named for James Madison (1751–1836), fourth president of the United States.

Manchester, Connecticut, was named for Manchester, England.

Manchester, New Hampshire, was settled in 1722 and named Derryfield. It later became known as Tyngstown, then Manchester, after England's chief industrial city.

Manhattan, New York, derives from the Wapinger name meaning "island of hills."

Manistee, Michigan, is an Ojibway name which has been variously translated as "crooked river," "lost river," "red river," "sound of the winds," or "spirit of the woods."

Manitowoc, Wisconsin, is an Algonquin name which means "abode of the Great Spirit."

Mansfield, Ohio, was named for Jared Mansfield, surveyor general of the United States, who plotted the town in 1808.

Manteo, North Carolina, was named for Chief Manteo, a Native American who was taken to England by Walter Raleigh in 1584.

Maple Heights, Ohio, was named for the many maple trees in the area. It was incorporated as a village in 1915.

Marietta, Georgia, was founded in 1834 and named for Marietta Cobb, whose husband was a judge.

Marietta, Ohio, was the first permanent European settlement in the state, although European traders had been in the area for over a hundred years. The town was named in honor of Queen Marie-Antoinette of France, in appreciation of the help France gave to the American colonies during the Revolutionary War.

Marion, Alabama, was named for Francis "Swamp Fox" Marion (1732–1795), a Revolutionary War general who mounted a successful guerrilla operation in the swamps of South Carolina, and was also a state senator. Settled in 1817, it is one of the oldest towns in the state. Its first name was Muckle Ridge.

Marion, South Carolina, was named for General Francis Marion (see *Marion, Alabama*).

Marlboro, New Jersey, was named for the marl beds that are found in the area. Discovered there in 1768, marl (soft, crumbly, clay soil) is used to make water softeners and fertilizer.

Martinsburg, West Virginia, is the gateway to the Shenandoah Valley. It was named for Colonel Thomas

Bryan Martin, nephew of Lord Fairfax, and a large landowner.

Mason City, Iowa,   was settled by Freemasons in 1853. Its earlier names were Shibboleth, Masonville, and Mason Grove. A large brick and tile industry is located there.

Massapequa Park, New York,   was named for the Massapequa, a band of Native Americans who lived there when the first European settlers arrived in the 1650s.

Massillon, Ohio,   was named for Jean Batiste Massillon, a preacher and writer at the French court of King Louis XVI. The town was founded in 1826 by James Duncan, whose wife was an admirer of Massillon's works.

Matanzas, Florida.   *Matanzas* is a Spanish word meaning "slaughters," "butcheries," or "massacres." The area got its name when, in 1565, the Spanish Catholic Pedro Menéndez mercilessly beheaded four hundred French Huguenot (Protestant) prisoners because they would not accept the Catholic religion. The spot has been called Matanzas ever since. Today there are a town, a park, and a memorial, all named Matanzas, on the site.

Maui, Hawaii,   is the name of both an island and a county including four other islands. It derives its name from the Polynesian demigod Maui, who fished the Hawaiian islands up out of the sea.

Maysville, Kentucky,   was laid out by Simon Kenton and John May. At first, the town was known as Limestone, but later the name was changed to honor John May.

Maywood, Illinois, was founded by Colonel William T. Nichols in 1869 and named for May Nichols, his daughter.

Medford, Oregon, was founded in 1833 and so named because it was on the middle ford of Bear Creek.

Melrose, Massachusetts, was named for Melrose, Scotland.

Memphis, Tennessee. General Andrew Jackson (1767–1845) and Judge John Overton once owned the land where Memphis now stands. They organized a small settlement there in 1819. Jackson laid out the town and named it Memphis, after Memphis, the ancient capital of Egypt. Jackson predicted that Memphis on the Mississippi would one day become a great city like Memphis on the Nile. Memphis was built on the site of an ancient Cherokee village.

Several years before Jackson named the place, the name Memphis had been suggested by James Winchester, a famous Revolutionary War soldier. He suggested the name because the Chickasaw Bluffs and the Mississippi River there reminded him of what he had read about Memphis on the Nile.

Mentor, Ohio, organized in 1815, was named for Hiram Mentor, an early settler.

Meridian, Mississippi, was named by a settler who thought that *meridian* meant "junction." It was founded in 1854 at the junction of the Mobile & Ohio and Vicksburg & Montgomery railroads.

Mesa, Arizona,   was settled in 1878 by Mormons who used prehistoric Native American canals for irrigation. The name comes from the Spanish word *mesa,* meaning "table," and refers to a high, flat tableland with sharply eroding sides. There are many mesas in the area.

Mesquite, Texas,   established in 1873, was named for nearby Mesquite Creek, which derived its name from the mesquite shrubs that once were plentiful in the area.

Methuen, Massachusetts,   was settled in 1642 and named for Sir Paul Methuen (1672–1757), later Lord Methuen.

Miami, Florida,   was founded in 1870 at the site of Fort Dallas, which the United States had built in the 1830s during the war against the Seminole. Prior to the building of the fort, the Seminole had lived there for over two thousand years. The Seminole word *mayaimi,* meaning "big water," which referred to Lake Okeechobee, was applied both to the indigenous people and to the city.

Middletown, Connecticut,   settled in 1650, was named for its position between Saybrook and Hartford.

Middletown, Pennsylvania,   was settled in 1752 and named for its location between Lancaster and Carlisle.

Milford, Connecticut, was settled in 1739 and named for Milford, Wales, or perhaps for a mill built in about 1640.

Milledgeville, Georgia, was laid out in 1803 and named for John Milledge, who was then governor.

Milwaukee, Wisconsin, derives from an Algonquin phrase, *mahn-a-wauk-ee,* meaning "gathering place by the waters." It was an important gathering place for the Fox, Mascouten, and Potawatomi. The first French Canadian settler moved into the area in 1818, and the indigenous people gave up their claim to the land in 1833. Later, several villages merged to form what is now Milwaukee.

Mineral Point, Wisconsin, derives its name from the lead and zinc found at a high rocky point between two creeks.

Minerva, Ohio, was named for Minerva Ann Taylor, the niece of its founder. She was the first white child born in the community.

Minneapolis, Minnesota, incorporated in 1856, derives its name from the Dakota word *minne,* meaning "water," and the Greek word *polis,* for "city." There are twenty-two natural lakes within the city limits.

Minnehaha Falls, Minnesota (geographical feature), derives its name from the Dakota words *minne haha,* meaning "water falls." The term is often translated as "laughing water," due to its seeming imitation of laughter. Longfellow wrote of these falls in his poem *The Song of Hiawatha.*

Minot, North Dakota, incorporated in 1887, was named in honor of Henry D. Minot (1859–1890), a railroad director and friend of Theodore Roosevelt.

Mishawaka, Indiana, founded in 1830, derives its name from the Potawatomi word *m'seh-wah-keeoki*, meaning "dead trees place" or "area cleared for settlement."

Missoula, Montana, was settled in 1841. It derives its name from a Salish term meaning "feared water" or "river of dread," believed to refer to Hell Gate Canyon, where the Blackfoot once ambushed the Salish.

Mobile, Alabama, derives its name from an indigenous band known as *Moila*, whose name possibly means "canoe paddlers." The French Canadian explorer Jean-Baptiste le Moyne, sieur de Bienville, gave it the name Mobile, which is a French corruption of Moila.

Modesto, California, derives its name from the Spanish word *modesto*, which means "modest." The town, founded in 1870 by the Central Pacific Railway, was named Modesto when railway director W. C. Ralston modestly refused to let them name the town in his honor.

Mohegan, Connecticut, was named for the Mohegan, also known as Mohican, a tribe of Native Americans.

Moline, Illinois, was established in 1843 by a milling firm. Its name derives from the French word *moulin*, meaning "mill." Today it is sometimes called the Plow City.

Monroe, Louisiana, was named for the *James Monroe,* the first steamboat to chug up the Ouachita River in 1819. It is said that the appearance of the boat so excited the people that they instantly changed the name of the community from Fort Miro to Monroe.

Monrovia, California, was named for William Monroe (1841–1925), who laid out the town in 1886.

Montclair, New Jersey, settled in 1666, is located on the west slope of the Wachtung mountains. The French term *mont clair* means "bright mountain."

Monteagle, Tennessee. The origin of the name is disputed. Some believe it was named for the eagles which are seen in the area (*mont* means "mountain"), while others think it was named for an English nobleman.

Monterey, California, was named in honor of Gaspar de Acevedey Zuñiga, conde de Monterey (1560–1606), viceroy of New Spain, who also gave his name to Monterey Bay and Monterey Pass.

Montevideo, Minnesota, was named for Montevideo, Uruguay. The name is derived from a Spanish term, whose Latin roots are *mons*, "mountain," and *video*, "to see."

Montgomery, Alabama, ★ was named for General Richard Montgomery (1738–1775), a hero of the Revolutionary War.

Monticello, Virginia, is the name of President Thomas Jefferson's estate home which, at the time it was built, was just outside Charlottesville. The mansion was built in 1770 atop a small mountain. Jefferson coined the name, which is of Latin derivation, meaning "little hill."

Montpelier, Vermont, ★ was named for the city of Montpellier, France, in recognition of France's help during the American Revolution. The French name means "bare mountain."

Morgantown, West Virginia, established in 1766, was named for its founder, Colonel Zackquill Morgan.

Moundsville, West Virginia. There are a number of prehistoric Native American mounds in West Virginia. Moundsville was named for one of these mounds, which is thought to be one of the largest on the continent. It rises to a height of seventy-nine feet, and is nine hundred feet around at the base. This great mound was apparently built to serve as a tomb for some high dignitary. Very little is known about the indigenous mound-building people.

Muncie, Indiana, founded in 1824, was named after the Munsee clan of the Leni-Lenapé, whose name is believed to mean "people of the stony country." The U.S. government purchased the land from the Munsee in 1820, and the Munsee were moved west.

Murfreesboro, Tennessee, was established in 1811 on a tract of land donated by William Lytle, a Revolutionary War soldier. The town was originally named Cannonsburg, after Newton Cannon, who later became governor of Tennessee. Some time later, the town was renamed in honor of Lytle's friend Colonel Hardy Murfree. Incorporated in 1817, Murfreesboro served as the state capital from 1818 to 1826.

Murray, Utah, was founded by Mormons in 1847. It was named for the governor of the Utah territory at that time, Eli H. Murray.

Muscatine, Iowa, was started as a trading post in 1833. It was first named Bloomington, but in 1850, it was renamed in honor of the Mascouten, a branch of the Potawatomi. *Mascouten* is an Algonquin name which is believed to mean "burning island."

Muscle Shoals, Alabama, was named for a variation in the spelling of mussels, which were abundant in the area.

Muskegon, Michigan, was established on Lake Michigan at the mouth of the Muskegon River. The name derives from the word *muskig*, an Ojibway word meaning "river and marshes."

Muskogee, Oklahoma, was founded in 1872 and named for the Muskogee, a branch of the Shawnee. Their name derives from the word *muskeg*, an Algonquin word meaning "grassy bog."

Nantucket, Massachusetts, is a summer resort town on Nantucket Island, off the coast of Massachusetts. The name derives from the Native American word *nanticut*, meaning either "far away land" or "sandy, sterile soil." Nantucket Island is eighteen miles south of Cape Cod and about fifty miles southeast of New Bedford.

Nashua, New Hampshire, was named for an indigenous village on the Nashua River. The name, Nashua, derived from the Native word *nashaway*, meaning "beautiful river with pebbly bottom," was also used to refer to the Native American tribe who inhabited the area.

Nashville, Tennessee, ★ was named for General Francis Nash (1742–1777), a Revolutionary War hero who was killed at the Battle of Germantown. The fort, built in 1780, was first called Fort Nashborough, using the old English suffix *borough*, meaning "city." After the American Revolution, this British name was deemed unacceptable, and the name was changed to the French form Nashville when the town was incorporated in 1784. Nashville has been the state capital since 1843 and is currently known throughout the nation as Music City because of its country music industry.

Natchez, Mississippi, was founded in 1716 by Jean-Baptiste le Moyne, sieur de Bienville, then governor of Louisiana, who named it Fort Rosalie. It was later named for the Natchez, a Caddo tribe, on whose land the town was built. *Natchez* is a Caddo word meaning "timber."

Natchitoches, Louisiana, was established in 1714 and named Fort Jean-Baptiste. It was later named for the Natchitoches, whose Caddo name means either "chestnut eaters," "chinquapin eaters," or "pawpaw eaters."

Needham, Massachusetts, was settled in 1680 and named for Needham, England.

New Albany, Indiana, was established in 1813 and named for the founders' hometown, Albany, New York.

New Bedford, Massachusetts, was first known as just Bedford, after the duke of Bedford, but the *New* had to be added to distinguish it from another Bedford in the same state.

New Bern, North Carolina, was settled in 1710 by a Swiss pioneer and named for his hometown, Berne, Switzerland.

New Brunswick, New Jersey, was settled in 1681 and originally named Inian's Ferry, after ferry operator John Inian. Later the town was named for King George I of England, who was also the duke of Brunswick.

New Castle, Pennsylvania, was settled in 1798 and named for the English industrial city Newcastle-upon-Tyne. John Stewart, the first settler, built an iron furnace there.

New Harmony, Indiana, was named for Harmony, Pennsylvania. English philosopher Robert Owen (1771–1858) established this as a utopian community in 1826.

New Haven, Connecticut, was so named because it was seen as a place of refuge by the settlers. Its original name was Quinnipiac, a Native American name referring to the Quinnipiac River, but English Puritans renamed it New Haven in 1640.

New Johnsonville, Tennessee, was first known as Johnsonville, after either a settler or Andrew Johnson.

A hundred years later, a new dam was built by the Tennessee Valley Authority, causing the area to be flooded. The residents moved several miles upstream, resettled, and called the town New Johnsonville. It was incorporated in 1949.

New Kensington, Pennsylvania, was named for Kensington, a borough of London, England.

New London, Connecticut, was founded by John Winthrop the Younger in 1646 and was at first known as Pequot. It took its name from London, England. The early settlers believed that some day it would become a great city like its namesake.

New Martinsville, West Virginia, was settled by Edward Doolin in 1780. At first it was named Martin's Fort to honor Presley Martin, who purchased the land and organized defensive measures after Doolin was killed by members of the indigneous population. The name was later changed to Martinsville, and the later still to New Martinsville, to avoid confusion with Martinsville, Virginia.

New Orleans, Louisiana, was founded in 1718 by Jean-Baptiste le Moyne, sieur de Bienville, governor of the French colony of Louisiana. Le Moyne made New Orleans the capital of the colony. He named it *La Nouvelle Orleans* ("new Orleans") after Philippe, duc d'Orléans (1674–1723), regent of France.

New Providence, New Jersey, was first named Turkey because there were so many wild turkeys in the region. In 1778, a gallery in a Presbyterian church collapsed and no one in the congregation was hurt. In gratitude, the citizens renamed the town Divine Providence, but in 1899, the name was changed to New Providence.

New Rochelle, New York, was founded by French Huguenot (Protestant) refugees in 1688, and named for La Rochelle, France. Now a residential suburb of New York, it is one of the richest cities per capita in the United States.

New York City, New York, was named for the state of New York.

Newark, California, was named for Newark, New Jersey, the hometown of one of its early settlers.

Newark, Delaware, derives its name from New Worke, the name of a parcel of land that was settled in 1688 by a Quaker who donated a piece of the land for a new meeting house.

Newark, New Jersey, was named for the biblical "New Ark." There is an English town named Newark, but this is not the origin of the name.

Newark, Ohio, was named for Newark, New Jersey, by General William C. Schenck, a former New Jersey resident.

Newberg, Oregon, was founded in 1869 by Quakers and named for Neuberg, Germany, birthplace of one of the settlers.

Newburgh, New York, was settled in 1709 and named for Newburgh, Scotland.

Newport News, Virginia, was possibly named in honor of Captain Christopher Newport, who led five expeditions to Jamestown, Virginia, from 1606 to 1612, and William Newce. In 1691, the village was called Newport Newce. The present name is believed to be a corruption.

Newport, Kentucky, was named in honor of Captain Christopher Newport, commander of the first ship to bring colonists to Jamestown, Virginia, in 1607.

Newton, Massachusetts, was originally part of Cambridge, but in 1688, it was separated and incorporated as New Towne. Later the name was shortened to Newton.

Niagara Falls, New York, derives from the Algonquin word *oni-aw-ga-rah*, meaning "thundering waters." The town was named after the falls.

Nome, Alaska, got its name due to a mapmaker's error. On a map a nearby cape was shown, with the notation "cape (name?)." The question mark was overlooked, the word *name* was read as Nome, and the name Cape Nome was born. The city of Nome took its name from the cape.

Norman, Oklahoma, was named in 1887 to honor Aubrey Norman, a Santa Fe Railway surveyor.

Norris, Tennessee, was named after Norris Dam, which got its name from George Norris of Nebraska.

Norristown, Pennsylvania, was organized as a township in 1730 and named for Isaac Norris, one of the chief landowners in the area. Norris and William Trent purchased the land from William Penn, Junior.

Northampton, Massachusetts, was settled in 1654 and named for Northampton, England. However, some suggest it was so named because it was the northernmost settlement on the Connecticut River.

Northfield, Minnesota, was named for John W. North, who founded the town in 1856.

Norwalk, Connecticut. Two origins have been put forward. One states Norwalk was named for the Norwalk, a band of Paugusset, whose name means "point of land." Another theory suggests that it was so named because its original boundary extended north from the sea for one day's walk.

Norwalk, Ohio, was named for Norwalk, Connecticut.

Novi, Michigan, was founded at the site of the sixth stagecoach stop on the old toll road out of Detroit. It derives its unusual name from the station sign No. VI, which came to be pronounced as a single word by travelers.

Oahu, Hawaii. The island of Oahu takes its name from the Hawaiian word *oahu*, meaning "gathering place." And a gathering place it is indeed! Today, with 1,031 people per square mile, the island is more densely populated than Japan or the British Isles. However, there are still parts of Oahu which look today as they did three hundred years ago, before Europeans first saw the island.

Oakland, California, was named for the many oak trees found there. It was named in 1851 by Horace W. Carpenter, operator of a transbay ferry service.

Ogden, Utah, was incorporated in 1851 and named for Peter S. Ogden, an early Hudson Bay co-agent.

Oklahoma City, Oklahoma, ★ derives from the Choctaw words *okla*, "people," and *homa*, "red," meaning "land of the red people." The name was later applied to the entire state.

Olympia, Washington, ★ is disputed. Some say it was named for the Olympic Mountains of the state, or the Greek Mount Olympus. Others say it was named after, or was at least influenced by, the book *Life of Olympia.*

Omaha, Nebraska, ★ was named for the Omaha, a Dakota tribe, whose name means "against the current" or "against the wind."

Orem, Utah, was named for Walter C. Orem, at the time president of the Salt Lake & Utah Electric Interurban Railroad.

Orlando, Florida, was named in honor of Orlando Reeves, who died in 1835 in a battle with Native Americans. The first settlers came to the area in 1837, but the city was not founded until 1844. The settlement grew up around Fort Collins, a U.S. Army post, and was first called Jernigen. It was renamed Orlando in 1857.

Orofino, Idaho. The Spanish name, meaning "fine gold," refers to the nearby gold-mining industry.

Oshkosh, Wisconsin, was named in 1840 for Oshkosh (1795–1858), a Menominee chief, whose name means "hoof" or "toe." The town was founded as a trading post, and was first known as Athens.

Ottumwa, Iowa, located on the Des Moines River, derives from the Algonquin word *ottumwa*, meaning "tumbling waters" or "rippling waters." First settled in 1843, it was named Louisville, but the name was changed two years later to Ottumwa.

Ouray, Colorado, was named for the great Utaw chief, Ouray (1820–1880), whose name means "arrow." In its early days, Ouray was a booming mining town, and mining is still carried on there today.

Owensboro, Kentucky, was named for Colonel Abraham Owen, a veteran of many Kentucky battles with Native Americans, who died in the Battle of Tippecanoe (1811). It was founded on the Ohio River around 1800 and named Yellow Banks, due to the color of the banks. In 1816, the town was officially laid out and named Rossboro after David Ross, a large property owner. Some years later it was renamed Owensboro.

Oxnard, California, was founded in 1898 and named for Henry Oxnard, who financed a sugar beet factory on the site.

Paducah, Kentucky, was laid out in 1827 by William Clark (1770–1838), who named it for his friend Paduke, a Chickasaw chief who lived in the area. William Clark, of Lewis and Clark, was a brother of George Rogers Clark, who earlier had been given the land as a grant.

Palm Beach, Florida. In 1873, a ship carrying a cargo of coconuts and wine was shipwrecked on a long, narrow island on the southern Florida coast. The crew had gotten into the wine and were so drunk that they lost control of the ship. Later, the shipwrecked coconuts sprouted and beautiful palm trees grew, giving the area its name. Today, the city's famous palms produce so many coconuts that West Palm Beach spends thousands of dollars annually just to dispose of them.

Palo Alto, California, was named after Palo Alto, Senator Leland Stanford's farm. The Spanish phrase *palo alto* means "tall trees," referring to the massive sequoias native to the area. Stanford University is located there.

Park Ridge, Illinois, was so named because it is located on a high ridge. Earlier names were Pennsville (1856) and Brickton.

Parkersburg, West Virginia, was settled in 1785 and named Neal's Station. It was later renamed Parkersburg in honor of Alexander Parker of Pittsburgh, who owned the land on which the town was built.

Parma, Ohio, was settled in 1816 by New England pioneers, and named Greenbriar. In 1826, it was renamed in honor of Parma, a province and city in Italy.

Pasadena, California, founded in 1855, got its name from the Ojibway term meaning "crown of the valley." However, some assert the name is an old Spanish term meaning "land of flowers."

Pascagoula, Mississippi, derives its name from the Caddo word *pascagoula*, meaning "singing river." The river produces a sound like that made by a swarm of bees.

Paterson, New Jersey,   was named in 1791 by the state legislature for William Paterson, former governor of New Jersey, U.S. senator, and associate justice of the U.S. Supreme Court.

Pawtucket, Rhode Island,   derives from the Algonquin word *pawtucket,* meaning "falls at the mouth of the river." Settled in 1671, it is now the second largest city in Rhode Island.

Peabody, Massachusetts,   was named for the great philanthropist, George Peabody (1795–1869). It was originally part of Salem and then became a part of the town of Danvers in 1752. In 1855, it was renamed South Danvers, then in 1868, it was given its present name.

Peacham, Vermont,   was chartered in 1763 and named for the heroine of *The Beggar's Opera* by John Gay (1685–1732), a popular show on both sides of the Atlantic.

Peculiar, Missouri.   Divergent stories account for the name of this town. A real estate agent was showing the land to a group of Spiritualists led by Jane Hawkins. When they came over a hill, Mrs. Hawkins remarked, "That's peculiar! It is the very place I saw in a vision in Connecticut." They purchased the land and named it Peculiar. Another story concerns the postmaster who, when requesting a name for the new post office, asked for "any name as long as it was different or peculiar."

Pekin, Illinois,   derives its name from the Chinese city Peking, now called Beijing. Settled in 1824, it was named Pekin in 1830 by Mrs. Nathaniel Cromwell, who falsely believed it was directly opposite Peking on the other side of the world.

Pennsauken, New Jersey,   combines the name Penn, the source of the name Pennsylvania, with the Algonquin word *sauk*, meaning "inlet."

Pensacola, Florida,   was named for the Pensacola. The Choctaw name *pensi okla*, meaning "hair people," was applied to the local Indigenous group, who wore their hair long.

Peoria, Illinois,   was named in 1825 for the Peoria, one of the five tribes of the Illinois confederacy. The name *Peoria* means "pack carriers."

Perth Amboy, New Jersey.   The town's original name, *Omboge*, is of Algonquin origin, and means "level ground." Amboy is an English corruption of Omboge. Later, Perth was added to the name in honor of the earl of Perth, an early proprietor.

Petersburg, Virginia,   was established on the site of Fort Henry in 1748 and named for Major Peter Jones, commander of Fort Henry in 1675.

Phenix City, Alabama,   was named in 1889 for the old Phenix Mills across the river in Columbus, Georgia. It had originally been given the name Brownsville in 1883.

Philadelphia, Pennsylvania,   was founded by William Penn (1644–1718) in 1682. He named it Philadelphia, which is a Greek name meaning "city of brotherly love," either for its pure meaning, or in honor of the biblical city of Philadelphia in Asia Minor. Philadelphia quickly became the largest city in colonial America.

Phoenix, Arizona, ★ began in 1866 when John Y. T. Smith started growing hay in the area to furnish fodder to Camp McDowell, an army post only a few miles away. When Jack Swilling passed through the area a year later, he was deeply impressed by the neglected canals that had been made by the prehistoric Native Americans. He asked himself the question, "Why could not these canals be restored and provide irrigation for the whole area, using water from nearby Salt River?"

He persuaded some people to invest in his Swilling Irrigation Canal Company, and before too long, several of the old canals had been opened again and several ranches created. Before a year had passed, crops had been harvested on the ruins of the ancient civilization.

An English scholar and adventurer, Darrel Duppa, visiting the young community, was reminded of the mythical bird, the phoenix. It was said that at the end of every five hundred years, when the bird was growing old, it completely burned itself by fire, then rose young again from its ashes. Seeing a new civilization springing up out of the ruins of the old one, Duppa suggested that this community be called Phoenix, in honor of the mythical bird.

Pierre, South Dakota, ★ was named after Fort Pierre, which was named for Pierre Chouteau, a French fur trader.

Pigeon Forge, Tennessee, was named after an iron foundry (forge) on the Little Pigeon River. The river got its name from the great numbers of pigeons which roosted there when the early settlers arrived.

Pisgah National Forest, in North Carolina takes its name from a Native American name meaning "the height."

Pittsburgh, Pennsylvania, was founded as Fort Pitt in 1758 on the site of the French Fort Duquesne. The British built the fort and named it in honor of William Pitt the Elder (1708–1778), war minister of England. A town was founded nearby in 1764 and named Pittsburgh, meaning "Pitt's village."

Plainview, Texas, began as a trading post, like many other U.S. cities. Surveyed in 1887, it owes its name to the fact that the surrounding terrain is flat and provides an unbroken view of the area.

Plattsburgh, New York, was named for Zephaniah Platt, one of the founders.

Plymouth, Massachusetts, was named for Plymouth, England, from whence the *Mayflower* had set sail.

Pocatelo, Idaho, was named for Pocatelo, a Bannock (Shoshone) chief, whose name means "the wayward." The railway purchased land from Chief Pocatelo to build a railroad through that part of the territory. The land was settled in 1882.

Pocomoke, Maryland, got its name from the Pocomoke River. The river's Algonquin name is believed to mean "broken ground."

Point Barrow, Alaska (geographical feature). In 1826, British commander Lt. Sir William Beechey was the first European to see the northernmost point in North America, which the Inuit called *Nuwuk*, meaning "the point." Beechey renamed it Point Barrow in honor of Sir John Barrow, secretary of the British admiralty.

Point Pleasant, West Virginia, was named by George Washington, who camped there in 1770 and apparently found it to be a pleasant place.

Pontiac, Michigan, was settled in 1882 and named for Ottawa Chief Pontiac (1720–1769), who united several Native American tribes with the French in a war against the British.

Portage, Wisconsin, derives from the French word *portage*, which refers to a strip of land over which canoeists must carry their canoes and supplies due to a hazard in the river. In Wisconsin, there is a mile-and-a-half strip of land between the Fox River, which flows into Lake Michigan through Green Bay, and the Wisconsin River, which empties into the Mississippi. If these two rivers had connected, explorers could have traveled by boat across the entire state. This area became a common *portage* for travelers going through Wisconsin.

Portland, Oregon, was founded in 1842 on the Willamette River, by Asa Lovejoy and Francis Pettygrove. Lovejoy wanted to name it for his hometown, Boston, Massachusetts, but Pettygrove wanted to name it for his hometown, Portland, Maine. They tossed a coin and Pettygrove won.

Portsmouth, New Hampshire, was incorporated in 1653 and named for Portsmouth, England.

Portsmouth, Ohio, was founded in 1803 by Major Henry Massie and named for Portsmouth, New Hampshire.

Pottstown, Pennsylvania, was laid out in 1754 and named for founder John Potts, an ironmaster.

Poughkeepsie, New York, derives from an Algonquin word which has been variously translated as "safe harbor," "waterfall," "pool at the base of the falls," or "reed-covered lodge by the little water place." It was settled by the Dutch in 1687.

Prairie du Chien, Wisconsin, located on the Mississippi River, is the second oldest town in the state. Its French name means "prairie of Dog," referring to Fox Chief Alim, whose name meant "dog."

Prophets Town, Indiana (historical battle ground), was named for Wabokieshiek (1794–1841), a Shawnee known as the Prophet due to his religious leadership, who was born in the area. Wabokieshiek served as an advisor to Black Hawk, who became involved in many wars with European settlers. Benjamin Harrison defeated Wabokieshiek at the Battle of Tippecanoe in 1811.

Providence, Rhode Island, ★ was named by founder Roger Williams (c. 1603–1683) in commemoration of God's merciful providence, meaning "divine guidance and care," in bringing the settlers to that place.

Provo, Utah, was settled by Mormons in 1849. At first it was called Fort Utah, but its named was changed in 1850 in honor of a trapper, Etienne Provost, whose name was alternately spelled Proveau, Provaux, Provot, then finally Provo. Today, Provo is the leading steel center in the West. The Provo River was also named for Etienne Provost.

Pueblo, Colorado, derives its name from *pueblo*, the Spanish word for "village." The town was founded by James Beckwourth in 1842 as a trading post.

Puget Sound, Washington (geographical feature), was explored by English Captain George Vancouver (1757–1798), in 1792, who named it for his companion, Lieutenant Peter Puget.

Pullman, Washington, was named for George Pullman (1831–1897), who was known for manufacturing railroad sleeping cars.

Quincy, Illinois, was settled in 1822 by John Wood, the twelfth governor of Illinois. The town was first named Bluffs. However, when President John Quincy Adams was inaugurated on March 4, 1825, Bluffs became the county seat, and was renamed in the new president's honor.

Quincy, Massachusetts, was settled in 1625 and named Mount Wollaston, later becoming known as Merry Mount. In 1792, the town was renamed in honor of Colonel John Quincy. Both John Adams and John Quincy Adams were born here.

Racine, Wisconsin, was founded by Gilbert Knapp, a lake captain, in 1834. At first, it was known as Port

Gilbert. In 1837 it was renamed Racine. Two sources have been suggested for the name. *Racine* is the French word for "root," and may refer to nearby Root River. Another possibility is the Algonquin word *pak-was-win*, meaning "place where wild rice grows."

Raleigh, North Carolina, ★ was named for Sir Walter Raleigh (1554–1618).

Randolph Air Force Base, Texas (military facility), was established in 1930 and named for Captain William M. Randolph, former adjutant of the Advanced Flying School, who was killed in a training flight.

Rapid City, South Dakota, was settled in 1876 by prospectors in the Black Hills and named for Rapid Creek, on which it was founded.

Reading, Massachusetts, was settled in 1639 and named for Reading, England.

Reading, Pennsylvania, was laid out by Thomas and Richard Penn, sons of William Penn, in 1748. It was named for Reading, England, where the Penn family had previously lived.

Red Wing, Minnesota, was named after the Dakota term *Koópoohoosha*, meaning "wing of the wild swan dyed red," a title given to Dakota chiefs.

Redlands, California, was named for the rich red soil found in the area. The town was founded in 1881 and developed as a citrus packing and distribution center.

Redwood City, California, was named for its giant redwood trees. The town was laid out in 1854 by Simon M. Mezes and first named Mezesville.

Reno, Nevada, was settled in 1860 and first named Lake's Crossing after M. C. Lake, who acquired the site where the community was built. It was later renamed for General Jesse Lee Reno (1823–1862) of Virginia, a Union officer who was killed in the Civil War.

Revere, Massachusetts, was settled in 1626 and named Rumney Marsh. It was renamed in 1871 in honor of Paul Revere (1735–1818).

Richfield, Minnesota, was first called Harmony, then Richland. In 1858, it was renamed Richfield, in reference to its rich farmland.

Richmond, Kentucky, was settled in 1784 and named for Richmond, Virginia.

Richmond, Virginia, ★ was founded in 1737 and named for Richmond-upon-Thames, England. Its history goes back to 1607, when the first successful English settlement in the New World was made at Jamestown, Virginia. At that time, an exploration party led by Christopher Newport and John Smith visited the site. In 1637, a trading post was established there, and in 1737, the site was surveyed and named.

Riverside, California, located on the side of the Santa Ana River, was laid out in 1870 and named Jurupa. It was later given a descriptive name.

Roanoke, Virginia, derives its name from the Delaware word *rewenoak*, meaning "shell money." The town was founded as a small pioneer settlement in 1841 and named Big Lick, for a nearby salt marsh where deer fed. In 1882, two railroads made a junction at Big Lick, and the name was changed to Roanoke. Today it is one of the largest cities in the state.

Robertsville, Ohio, was laid out in 1842 by a Frenchman, Joseph Robard, and named Robertsville for the English version of Robard.

Rochester, Minnesota, was settled in 1854 and named for Rochester, New York.

Rochester, New Hampshire, was incorporated in 1722 and named for Lawrence Hyde, earl of Rochester.

Rochester, New York, was named for Colonel Nathaniel Rochester (1752–1831), who surveyed the site in 1803. It was first called Fallstown, since it is near the Upper Falls. In 1811, lots were sold to settlers, and before a year had passed, the town had grown to five hundred. It was renamed Rochesterville, after the colonel, then later shortened to Rochester.

Rock Hill, South Carolina, was established in 1851 and named for a flint hill in the area.

Rock Island, Illinois, was named for an island in the Mississippi River, near the mouth of the Rock River. It was founded in 1835 as Stephenson, and renamed Rock Island in 1841. During the Civil War, it was used to house Confederate prisoners of war.

Rockford, Illinois, was founded on the Rock River in 1834 by settlers from New England. At first it was called Midway, because it was the site of a coach stop halfway between Chicago and Galena. It was later named for the ford across the Rock River, which derived its name from its rocky bottom.

Rockville, Maryland, was settled during the Revolutionary War and named in 1803 for nearby Rock Creek. Earlier names were Hungerford's Tavern, Montgomery Courthouse, and Williamsburg.

Rogersville, Tennessee. The little town of Rogersville, in the hills of eastern Tennessee, was founded in 1796 as a wedding gift to Joseph Rogers and his bride. Davy Crockett's grandparents had a cabin on Crockett Creek, which runs through the town. Members of the Crockett and Rogers families are buried in the town cemetery.

Rome, Georgia, was named for the ancient city of Rome, Italy. It was founded in 1834 as a clearinghouse for cotton and other farm produce between Georgia and Tennessee.

Roswell, New Mexico, lies in the Pecos Valley in the southwestern part of the state. It was founded by Van C. Smith in 1871 as a trading post. When it was time to name the new post office, he named it for his father, Roswell Smith.

Rotterdam, New York, was named for Rotterdam, the Netherlands. It has the same official seal.

Royal Oak, Michigan, founded in 1819, took its name from the famous Royal Oak of Scotland, a giant oak tree, the foliage of which is said to have hidden Charles II. Governor Lewis Cass (1782–1866) named the town for a large oak tree that reminded him of the Royal Oak.

Rutland, Vermont,   was incorporated in 1893 and named for John Manners, third duke of Rutland (1696–1779).

Sacramento, California, ★   derives its name from the Sacramento River, which was named for the Spanish word *sacramento*, meaning "blessed sacrament" or "holy communion." It was here, at Sutter's Mill, that gold was found on January 24, 1848, leading to the 1849 Gold Rush.

Saginaw, Michigan,   derives from the Sauk word *saginaw*, meaning "mouth of the river." The Sauk had a village on the site, which was abandoned and later occupied by the Ojibway. A fur trading post was established nearby in 1816, from which the town grew. Saginaw is located on Saginaw River, which empties into Saginaw Bay.

Saint Augustine, Florida,   was first sighted in 1585 by Spanish explorer Pedro Menéndez de Avilés, on the feast day of Saint Augustine.

Saint Cloud, Minnesota,   was settled in the 1850s by Ole Bergeson, a Norwegian. In 1853, John L. Wilson of Maine paid Bergeson $250 for 325 acres, and founded the town. He named it for St. Cloud, Napoleon I's palace near Paris, France.

Saint Louis, Missouri,   was founded in 1764 by two French fur traders, Pierre Laclede and René Auguste

Chouteau, who established a trading post on the site. It was named for Louis IX, a French king who had been made a saint in 1297.

Saint Paul, Minnesota, ★ was named for Saint Paul, to whom in 1841 Father Lucian Galtier dedicated a log church, around which a settlement grew.

Saint Petersburg, Florida, was named for St. Petersburg, Russia, birthplace of founder Peter A. Demens, who built a railroad from central Florida to the area in 1888.

Salem, Massachusetts, was founded in 1626 by Roger Conant, who named it after the biblical city of Jerusalem, which in old Hebrew means "city of peace." The first Congregational Church in the New World was organized here in 1629.

Salem, New Jersey, established in 1675 by Quaker John Fenewick, derives its name from the Hebrew word *shalom*, meaning "peace."

Salem, Oregon, ★ derives its name from the Hebrew word *shalom*, meaning "peace." It was settled in 1840 by Methodist missionaries led by Jason Lee. Its original name was *Chemekata*, an Athapascan term meaning "place of rest." The missionaries kept the same idea but used the old Hebrew word.

Salina, Kansas, was founded in 1858 by abolitionists, who named it for the Saline River. *Saline* is a French name meaning "salt flats."

Salinas, California, was settled in 1856 and named for the Salinas River. *Salinas* is a Spanish name meaning "salt marshes."

Salt Lake City, Utah, ★ was named after Great Salt Lake, the largest inland body of salt water in the New World. Mormon leader Brigham Young surveyed the site in 1847 and laid out the town. His plan was impressive. The blocks are ten acres square and the streets are 132 feet wide. Authorities have labeled Salt Lake City one of the most beautiful and well planned cities in the United States.

San Angelo, Texas, was founded in 1869 and named Over-the-River. It was later renamed for Santa Angelo, the founder's sister-in-law, who was a nun, but the name was masculinized.

San Antonio, Texas, is located at the headwaters of the San Antonio River, and some authorities think the town was named for it. There are others, however, who say that San Antonio was named for Saint Anthony of Padua, Italy. Permanent settlement did not begin until 1718, when the Spanish built the Mission of San Antonio de Velero, now known as the Alamo.

San Bernardino, California, was named by Spanish missionaries for Saint Bernardino of Siena, Italy. Mormons laid out the town in 1852.

San Carlos, California. Explorers first sighted San Francisco Bay on the feast day of Saint Charles of Borromeo. San Carlos is the Spanish form of Saint Charles. The town was laid out in 1888 by the Southern Pacific Railroad.

San Diego, California. In 1602, Spanish explorer Sebastian Vizcaíno (c. 1550–1616) spent nearly a year on the California coast. He gave many places the names they still bear, including San Diego, Catalina Island, Santa Barbara, Carmel, and Monterey Bay. On November 10, Vizcaíno went ashore, and two days later, on the feast day of San Diego de Alcala (Saint James of Alcala), he held the first Catholic service in California. Vizcaíno then named the bay in honor of the saint of his flagship, which also carried the name *San Diego*.

San Fernando, California, was named for the *Mission San Fernando Rey de España*, which was established in 1797. The name means "Saint Ferdinand, king of Spain," and refers to King Ferdinand III of Castile and León, the royal houses of Spain.

San Francisco, California, was named for Saint Francis. In 1595, the Spanish explorer Sebastian Rodrigues Germeno discovered the bay and named it *Puerto de San Francisco* ("Port of Saint Francis"). This established the name San Francisco for the region.

San Joaquin Valley, California, takes its name from the San Joaquin River, which was named in 1805 in honor of Saint Joachim, legendary father of the Virgin Mary. Joaquin is the Spanish form of Joachim.

Sandusky, Ohio, derives from the Wyandot word *otsaandosti*, meaning "cool water" or "pure water." Located on Sandusky Bay, at the entrance to Lake Erie, the site was first settled as Fort Sandusky by the British in 1761.

Sanford, Florida, was named for Henry S. Sanford (1823–1891), a former minister in Belgium, who purchased nearby land to grow citrus fruits. Settlers came in 1836, and the place was named Sanford in 1877.

Sanford, Maine, was named for the children of settler John Sanford (d. 1653).

Santa Ana, California, at the base of the Santa Ana River, was named after Saint Anne, the mother of the Virgin Mary. The site was laid out by William Spurgeon in 1869.

Santa Barbara, California, was named in 1602 by Spanish explorer Sebastian Vizcaíno (c. 1550–1616), for Saint Barbara, patron saint of mariners.

Santa Claus, Indiana, was laid out in 1846 and named Santa Fe. It became necessary to change the name when it was discovered that there was another city by that name in Indiana. It is said that on Christmas Eve, 1852, while residents were trying to find a name, the local Santa Claus walked in and they unanimously agreed on the name. Approximately one million pieces of mail addressed simply to "Santa Claus" are received by this post office during each Christmas season.

Santa Fe, New Mexico, ★ is a shortened form of the original Spanish name, *La Villa Real de la Santa Fe de San Francisco de Assisi,* meaning "the royal town of the holy faith of Saint Francis of Assisi." *Santa Fe* means "holy faith."

Santa Monica, California, was named by Father Crespi, a Spanish missionary who camped on the site on Saint Monica's Day in 1769.

Savannah, Georgia, was founded in 1733 by James Oglethorpe, who selected a site on the Yamacraw Bluff overlooking a wide expanse of flat country that the Spanish call *savannah.* Savannah comes from the Carib word *zabana,* meaning "grassy plain" or "marsh." The Yamacraw Bluff was named for a nearby Creek village.

Schenectady, New York, founded by the Dutch in 1661, derives its name from the Mohawk word *schenectady,* meaning "near the pines."

Scottsbluff, Nebraska, was named for Hiram Scott, a fur trader who died in the area in 1828. Washington Irving, in his "Adventures of Captain Bonnebille," tells how he died. Scott became ill, and his companions stopped until he could get well enough to resume the journey. They left him for what was supposed to be just a few minutes to search for edible roots, but while they were searching for food they found the trail of some travelers who had preceded them a short time before. Thinking that they might overtake them, they left Scott and hastened onward. They finally did overtake the party, but concealed their faithless desertion of Scott by saying that he had died of disease.

The next summer, these deserters, in company with others, were visiting the area when they found the bleached bones and grinning skull of Scott. The poor man had crawled sixty miles before he died.

The eight-hundred-foot bluff at Scottsbluff is now known as Scott's Bluff Monument. It has a museum of artifacts that belonged to pioneers in the region.

Scranton, Pennsylvania, was settled in 1851 and named for Joseph H. Scranton, one of the founders of the Lackawanna Iron and Steel Company. Earlier names were Lackawanna, Harrison, and Scrantonia.

Seattle, Washington, was named, by suggestion of Dr. David S. Maynard, an early businessman, in honor of Chief Sealth (1786–1866), a Suquamish who was friendly to early settlers in the 1850s. The settlers referred to Chief Sealth as Seattle and were enthusiastic about naming the settlement in his honor. However, Sealth objected to this because he was afraid it would offend his guardian spirit, but finally he consented and the future city took his name.

Chief Sealth believed that in the afterlife his spirit would be troubled each time his name was spoken. For that reason, it is said, he asked the residents of Seattle to give him gifts to repay him in advance for his troubles in the next life.

Sebago, Maine, was named for Sebago Lake, whose Abenaki name means "big lake."

Selma, Alabama, was settled in 1815 and named for the Selma Land Company, which derived its name from James MacPherson's poem, "The Song of Selma." The *selma* in the poem means "high throne" and was applied to a high northern bank of the Alabama River. An earlier name for the town was Moore's Bluff.

Selmer, Tennessee, was named for Selma, Alabama, but P. H. Thrasher, who named it, misspelled it when submitting the name to the Post Office Department. Selmer became the county seat in 1890.

Sevierville, Tennessee, was named for John Sevier, first governor of Tennessee.

Seward, Alaska, was named in honor of Secretary of State William H. Seward (1801–1872), who used his influence to get the United States to purchase Alaska from Russia.

Sharon, Pennsylvania, settled in 1802, was named for the biblical plain of Sharon in Palestine, due to its similar flat geography.

Sheboygan, Wisconsin, was settled as a lumber village in 1835. Its name derives from *sheboygan*, an Ojibway word meaning "rumbling underground," which referred to the Sheboygan River.

Shelbyville, Tennessee, was laid out in 1810 and named for Colonel Isaac Shelby (1750–1826), a veteran of the Revolution and the War of 1812, known for defeating the British at King's Mountain in 1780.

Shepardstown, West Virginia. The first log cabin in what is now West Virginia was built here in 1726. German settlers slowly began to move into the area, and later it was named New Mecklenberg. In 1732, Thomas Shepard arrived and bought a one-thousand-acre estate, and in 1764, he laid out the town, which took its name from him. Shepardstown is thought to be the oldest European settlement in West Virginia.

Sheridan, Wyoming, was named for General Phillip Henry Sheridan (1831–1888), a famous Civil War hero. J. D. Loucks, who fought under Sheridan in the war, founded and named the town.

Shreveport, Louisiana, was named for Captain Henry Miller Shreve (1785–1851), who cleared the Red River of its debris so that it became navigable.

Europeans who first came to the area found the Red River blocked with trees and mud. It had probably started hundreds of years ago, when a heavy storm upstream tore down thousands of trees and jumbled them together in a twisted mass where Natchitoches now stands. As time passed, more snags and trunks piled behind the original mass. These were pushed together tighter and tighter until they were twenty-five feet deep in some places. The roots, tree trunks, and mud were pressed together so tightly that the whole mass was almost as hard as concrete. The water backed up for 214 miles. Millions of acres of good farm land were covered with swamps and marshes. For a thousand miles, the Red River was cut off from steamboat traffic, and the whole valley remained unsettled because of this great blockage.

In 1833, Captain Shreve brought his snag boat *Archimedes* to the Red River. This was a double-hulled boat which Shreve had developed to batter out trees and snags on the Mississippi. After two months of work, seventy-five miles had been cleared, and Shreve and other investors purchased a million acres from the Caddo. A town was then founded and named Shreve's Landing, later changing its name to Shreveport in 1835. By 1839, after five years of work, the river was completely clear. Government engineers had estimated the work would cost three million dollars, but Shreve had done it for a mere three hundred thousand.

Silver Spring, Maryland, was named for the Silver Spring, which was named for the silvery mica flakes that gleamed on its bottom.

Sioux City, Iowa, was named for the Dakota, whom the French called *Sioux*, meaning "vipers" or "enemies." It was first settled in 1849 as Thompsonville.

Sioux Falls, South Dakota, was founded in 1857 and named for the falls on the Big Sioux River.

Sitka, Alaska, derives its name from the Tlingit term *sitka*, meaning "by the sea." Sitka is the Tlingit name for Baranof Island, on which the city of Sitka is located.

Skokie, Illinois, takes its name from the Potawatomi word *skokie*, meaning "swamp" or "marsh." It was settled in 1834 and was originally known as Niles Carter.

Smuggler's Notch, Vermont (geographical feature), was given its name because a large volume of illegal goods and cattle was hidden from the British there during the War of 1812.

Smyrna, Delaware, was settled in 1769 and named for the biblical city of Smyrna, an ancient Greek seaport.

Smyrna, Georgia, was settled in 1832 and named for the biblical city of Smyrna.

Somerset, Kentucky, was established in 1801 and named after Somerset, Pennsylvania.

Somerset, Pennsylvania, was named after the duke of Somerset.

Somerville, Massachusetts, was settled in 1630 and later named for Captain Richard Somers (1778–1804), a naval hero in the Tripolitan War (1801–1805).

South Bend, Indiana, was named for the great bend in the St. Joseph River on which the city was built. Previous names were Big Street, Joseph Station, and Southland.

Spartanburg, South Carolina, established in 1785, is located in Spartan County. Both places were named for the Spartan Regiment, a South Carolina militia that fought in the Revolutionary War. The regiment took its name from the Spartans, warriors of Sparta, Greece, who were renowned for their military prowess in the fifth century B.C.E.

Spokane, Washington, was named for the Spokan, a Salish band whose name is believed to mean "people of the sun." It was founded as a trading post in 1810 near the falls in the Spokane River, and was settled in 1871 as Spokane Falls.

Springfield, Arkansas, was first settled in 1850 and grew up around a spring. Its earlier name was Spring-in-the-Dale.

Springfield, Illinois, ★ was settled in 1818 and named for a local spring which emptied into nearby Spring River.

Springfield, Massachusetts, was incorporated in 1641 and named for Springfield, Essex, England. The first federal armory was built here, and the Springfield rifle was developed here.

Springfield, Ohio, was settled in 1799 by James Demint of Kentucky. It was named for the many nearby springs.

Springfield, Vermont, was chartered in 1761 and named for Springfield, Massachusetts.

Stamford, Connecticut, was founded in 1641 by pioneers from Wethersfield, Connecticut, who named the settlement for Stamford, England.

Steubenville, Ohio, was founded in 1765 by Jacob Walker and was first known as Fort Steuben. It was named for Prussian officer Friedrich Wilhelm Augustin, baron von Steuben (1730–1794), who, as inspector general of the Continental army, trained many American soldiers during the Revolutionary War.

Stillwater, Minnesota, lies on the boundary between Minnesota and Wisconsin, near the mouth of the St. Croix River, at a point where the river widens into a lake, thus giving the town its name.

Stockton, California, was named in honor of Commodore Robert Stockton (1795–1866) of the U.S. Navy. Founded in 1847, its first name was Tuleburg. Stockton is California's only inland port.

Stratford, Connecticut, settled in 1639, was named for Stratford-upon-Avon, England, hometown of William Shakespeare. The city hosts a Shakespeare festival in a reproduction of the Globe Theatre.

Sumpter, South Carolina, founded in 1785, was named for Brigadier General Thomas Sumpter, an officer in the Revolutionary War.

Superior, Wisconsin, is a port on Lake Superior, and derives its name from the lake.

Syracuse, New York, was named for Syracuse, one of the most powerful cities of the ancient Greek world.

Tacoma, Washington, was settled in 1864 and first called Commonwealth City. It was later given the name Tacoma, derived from the Salish name for Mount Rainier. The word *tacoma* is believed to mean simply "mountain."

Tallahassee, Florida, ★ got its name from the Creek words *talwa* and *hasi*, meaning "town" and "old." Spanish explorer Hernando De Soto (1500–1542) visited a Creek village on the site in 1539 or 1540. Tallahassee was the only Confederate state capital that was not captured during the Civil War.

Tampa, Florida, derives its name from the Cree word *itimpi*, meaning "near it," or possibly "split wood." It is thought that this was the name of a Cree village which was visited by Spanish explorers in the 1500s. The Seminole successfully resisted European attempts to settle in the area until 1823, when a contingent of U.S. troops established a fort. Eight years later, a settlement was founded and given the name Tampa.

Tarpon Springs, Florida, was founded in 1876 and named because of the mistaken belief that tarpon laid their eggs in the nearby bayou (stream). The fish were actually mullet.

Taunton, Massachusetts, was named for Taunton, England.

Teaneck, New Jersey, was settled by the Dutch and named for the Teneyck (or Ten Eyck) family.

Ten Sleep, Wyoming,   got its distinctive name because, according to a Native American method of measuring distance, it was ten nights, or "ten sleeps," away from both Fort Laramie and Yellowstone.

Terre Haute, Indiana,   derives from the French term *terre haute*, meaning "high land." The town was laid out in 1816, and several important railroads came through the area, stimulating its early growth.

Texarkana, Arkansas,   and **Texarkana, Texas**, settled in 1874, took their names from a combination of *Tex*as, *Ark*ansas, and Louisi*ana*. Known as the Twin Cities, the two cities lie on the boundary between Arkansas and Texas, twenty-five miles north of the Louisiana border.

Tishomingo, Oklahoma,   was the capital of the Chickasaw Nation from 1856 to 1937. The city was named after Chief Tishomingo (1733?–1837?), whose name means "assistant chief." Tishomingo was the principal leader after Chief Ishtehotopa.

Toledo, Ohio,   was named for Toledo, Spain. It is believed that settlers named the town obliquely in honor of popular author Washington Irving (1783–1859), who was minister to Spain from 1842 to 1846.

Tombstone, Arizona,   was named by prospector Ed Schieffelin, who moved there in the 1860s. Soldiers tried to keep him from going to the area, telling him that "all he would find instead of silver would be his own tombstone." He named the site Tombstone when he hit his first strike in 1870.

Tonawanda, New York,   derives from the Iroquois word *tonawanda*, meaning "swift running water." Near the Niagara River, the town was settled in 1823 by people who came to work on the Erie Canal.

Topeka, Kansas, ★ derives its name from *topeka*, the Dakota word meaning "good place to dig potatoes (roots)." The site was settled by abolitionists from Lawrence, Kansas, in 1854.

Torrance, California, was founded in 1911 by Jared Sidney Torrance and named for him.

Torrington, Connecticut, was named for Torrington, Devonshire, England. Settled in 1735, its earlier names were Orlana Village and Mast Swamp.

Trenton, New Jersey, ★ was named for William Trent, a Philadelphia businessman, who laid out the town. First settled in 1679 by Mahlon Stacy, it was known as The Falls, due to the eight-foot waterfall on the nearby river. In 1714, Stacy sold eight hundred acres to William Trent, who became chief justice of the colony of New Jersey. In 1719, it was renamed Trent Town, later changed to Trenton.

Troy, New York, was settled by the Dutch in 1707, who named it Vanderheyden's Ferry in honor of a major landowning family in the area. In 1789, it was renamed for the ancient city of Troy in Asia Minor.

Tucson, Arizona, derives its name from the Spanish version of the Papago words *chuk shon*, meaning "black base," referring to the volcanic rock in the area.

Tulsa, Oklahoma. When the Creek first came to this region, they called their small settlement *Talwa Hasi*, meaning "old town," in honor of their former home in Alabama. Tulsa, Alabama, is now known as Tallahassee. Tulsa, Oklahoma, became the boundary point between the Cherokee, Osage, and Creek nations. Today there are more than eight hundred oil company plants and offices in the city.

Tuscaloosa, Alabama, derives from the Choctaw words *tashka*, "warrior," and *lusa*, "black." The town is believed to have been named for Chief Tuskalusa, who flourished during the time of De Soto (1538). Today the name is applied both to the town and, in translation, to the Black Warrior River.

Tyler, Texas, was named for John Tyler (1790–1862), tenth president of the United States.

Union City, New Jersey, is made up of several towns that united, hence the name. The earliest settlement was 1740.

Urbana, Illinois, laid out in 1805, derives its name from the Latin word *urbana*, meaning "urban" or "citified," and by extension, "politeness" or "refinement."

Utica, New York, was settled by Dutch and German immigrants. The name Utica was chosen by drawing the name out of a hat, and comes from the ancient city of Utica in North Africa.

Valdosta, Georgia, was named in 1860 after Valdosta, the plantation of Governor G. M. Troup. *Valdosta* is an old Italian name meaning "valley of beauty."

Vallejo, California, was named for General Mariano G. Vallejo, who offered land for the new state capital.

His offer was not accepted, but the town that grew up there took his name.

Vancouver, Washington, was named for Captain George Vancouver (1757–1798), an English explorer who mapped the west coast of North America.

Ventura County, California, took its name from the San Buenaventura (Saint Bonaventure) Mission, founded in 1782.

Vernon Parish, Louisiana (county equivalent), derives its name from George Washington's estate, Mount Vernon. However, some assert that it was named for a well-liked racehorse by that name.

Vicksburg, Mississippi, was settled by the French in 1718. It was named in 1825 in honor of the Reverend Newitt Vick, a Methodist minister. Earlier names were Nogales and Walnut Hills.

Victory, Wisconsin, was named by the victors of the Battle of Bad Axe (1832). The U.S. militia met the Sauk on the banks of the Mississippi, and when the Sauk tried to surrender, the militia all but wiped them out.

Vincennes, Indiana, was settled shortly after 1700, making it one of the oldest European settlements outside the thirteen colonies. In 1732, the French built a fort on the site and placed it under the command of Françqis-Marie Bissot, sieur de Vincennes, who was killed by the Indigenous people in 1736. Soon after that, the town was named in his honor.

Waco, Texas, was established in 1849 and named for Tawakoni, the Caddo village on which the town was founded. *Tawakoni* means "river bend among red sand hills." There are also claims that the name derives from *wehico*, a Native American variation on "Mexico," or *wako*, the Seminole word for "blue heron."

Walla Walla, Washington, derives from the Shahaptian (Nez Percé) term *wallawalla*, meaning "little river" or "place of many waters." The region has many streams. Today, Walla Walla serves as the trading and shipping center for the truck farms and ranches of southeastern Washington and northeastern Oregon.

Wallingford, Connecticut, was founded in 1640 and called East River, then New Haven Village. Later it was renamed after Wallingford, England.

Wantagh, New York, was named for Wantage, England, birthplace of King Alfred the Great (871–899). The reason for the change in spelling is unclear.

Warren, Arkansas, was founded in 1842 and named for Warren Bradley, a slave who was owned by the leader of the settlers. Bradley was a faithful bodyguard, and the town was named out of gratitude for his service.

Warren, Michigan, organized in 1837, was named for Joseph Warren (1741–1775), a Revolutionary War hero. Earlier names were Hickory Township and Alba.

Warrensburg, Missouri, was settled in 1833 and named for Martin Warren, a Revolutionary War hero.

Wartburg, Tennessee, was settled by Germans and Swiss and named for Wartburg, Germany, a well-known residence of religious reformer Martin Luther.

Warwick, Rhode Island, was named for Robert Rich, earl of Warwick (1587–1658), who granted to settlers a charter of self-government here in 1644.

Washington, District of Columbia, was named for George Washington (1732–1799), who chose the exact spot for the city in 1791. Unlike most American cities, Washington was designed and laid out before the first buildings were erected.

The location of our nation's capital was the result of a compromise. The South did not want the capital to be in Philadelphia, because the Quakers who lived there favored abolition. The North did not want the capital to be in a slave state, because this would make it look as if the United States favored slavery. So the location was worked out as a compromise on the recommendation of Alexander Hamilton in 1790.

Washington is on land that was given by the state of Maryland for that purpose. It is about seventy square miles. Virginia gave about thirty square miles for the capital city but later asked for the land to be returned. So today all of Washington is on land that was given by the people of Maryland. The District of Columbia, a separate political entity not within either state, was named for Christopher Columbus.

Washington, Georgia, was the first community of any size to be named for George Washington.

Washington, Kentucky, and **Washington, New Hampshire**, were named for George Washington.

Washington, North Carolina, is said to be the first city named for George Washington.

Waterbury, Connecticut, was settled in 1674 and given its name in 1686 because of the abundant waterways providing drainage through its steep granite hills and slopes.

Waterloo, Iowa, was settled in 1845. It is thought that the name was taken from a postal directory when the community applied for a post office "because it had the right ring to it," or that it was named in commemoration of the Battle of Waterloo (1815).

Waukegan, Illinois, was named for Waukegan Creek, which derives its name from the Illinois word *waukegan*, meaning "place of shelter." The place was called Little Fort by the French, who visited the area in 1695.

Waukesha, Wisconsin, was settled in 1834 and named Prairieville. It was later named Waukesha after *Wakusheg*, a Potawatomi name for the Fox tribe.

Wausau, Wisconsin, was settled in 1839 as a sawmill town and named Big Bull Falls. In 1872 it was renamed *Wausau*, which is an Ojibway word meaning "faraway place."

Waverly, Tennessee, was named for *Waverley*, Sir Walter Scott's first popular novel. The town was named by Stephenson Pavette, one of Scott's admirers.

Wayne, Michigan, was settled in 1836 and named for General "Mad Anthony" Wayne (1745–1796), a Revolutionary War officer. Mad Anthony got his nickname due to his many daring tactics during the war. He achieved several victories over the British and later over the Native Americans, and many towns were named in his honor.

Wayne, New Jersey; Waynesboro, Pennsylvania; and **Waynesboro, Virginia**, were all named for General "Mad Anthony" Wayne.

Webster City, Iowa, settled in 1850, was named either for the owner of a stagecoach line between Fort Dodge, Iowa, and Belmont, Wisconsin, or for Daniel Webster (1782–1852), a famous American statesman and orator.

Webster County, Mississippi, was named for Daniel Webster.

Weirton, West Virginia, was settled during the Revolutionary War and later named for the Weir brothers, who started a tin factory there in 1909. Weirton has a long history of iron making.

Wellesley, Massachusetts, was named for Welles, the estate of Horatio Hunnewell, which was named for his wife, Isabelle Welles Hunnewell.

West Allis, Wisconsin, was settled in 1880 and named for the Allis-Chambers Manufacturing Company, a heavy-machinery maker that built a plant there. Its earlier name was North Greenfield.

West Bend, Wisconsin, was founded in 1845 and named for a bend in the Milwaukee River on which it is located.

Weymouth, Massachusetts, was settled in 1622, and upon incorporation in 1635 was named for Weymouth, England.

Wheaton, Illinois, was settled by the Wheaton brothers, Warren and Jesse, who had migrated there from Pomfret, Connecticut.

Wheeling, West Virginia, took its name from the Native American *wie* or *wihl*, and *ling*, which all mean "head." It is said that the first Europeans who entered the area were killed, and their heads were placed on poles to warn away other invaders. The town was settled by the Zane family in 1769.

White Plains, New York, was first settled in 1735. At that time, the Simwanoy name for the area was *Quarropas*, meaning "white marshes," which referred to the white balsam growing there. When the town was organized in 1866, it became known as White Plains.

White Sulpher Springs, West Virginia, was named for its heavily sulphured mineral springs, which have since made it a health resort.

Whittier, California, was settled by Quakers in 1887 and named for Quaker poet John Greenleaf Whittier (1807–1892).

Wibaux, Montana, was named for prominent citizen Pierre Wibaux, who at one time owned seventy-five thousand head of cattle.

Wichita, Kansas was named for the Wichita, a Caddo tribe. The word *wichita* means simply "human being."

Wichita Falls, Texas, was named for the Wichita tribe.

Wilkes-Barre, Pennsylvania, was named for John Wilkes and Isaac Barré, both British members of Parliament. Wilkes and Barré were outspoken defenders of the American colonies and were heroes to the Connecticut settlers who founded the town in 1769. Two of the families also named their sons after Wilkes and Barré.

Wilkinsburg, Pennsylvania, was named in honor of Judge William Wilkins, who was also a senator and secretary of war under President John Tyler. Settled in 1798, its earlier names were McNairsville and Rippeysville.

Williamsburg, Virginia, was settled in 1633 and named in honor of King William III of England. Home of William and Mary College, its earlier name was Middle Plantation.

Williamson, West Virginia, was established in 1892 and named for one of its well-known citizens, Wallace J. Williamson.

Williamsport, Pennsylvania, was founded in 1795. It is believed to have been named for William Russell, operator of a local ferry service.

Wilmette, Illinois, was settled in 1869 by a French Canadian, Antoine Ouilmette, who named the town in honor of his Potawatomi wife, Archange Ouilmette.

Wilmington, Delaware, was settled in 1728 and named New Liverpool, but when it was incorporated in 1739, it was renamed in honor of Spenser Compton, earl of Wilmington.

Wilmington, North Carolina,   was first known as New Town, then Newton. It was later named for the earl of Wilmington.

Wilson, North Carolina,   was incorporated in 1849 and named in honor of Brigadier General Louis P. Wilson (1789–1847), a hero of the Mexican War (1846–1848).

Winchester, Connecticut,   was settled in 1750 and named for Winchester, England.

Winchester, Kentucky,   was founded in 1782 and named for Winchester, England, former home of one of the founders.

Winchester, Massachusetts,   settled in 1640, was named for businessman Colonel William P. Winchester of Watertown. Earlier names were Charleston, South Woburn, and Black Horse Village.

Winfield, Kansas,   was founded in 1870 and named for ostentatious military leader General Winfield Scott (1786–1866).

Winnemucca, Nevada,   was named for Winnemucca (1844–1891), a Paiute educator, whose European name was Sara Hopkins. She worked as a teacher and interpreter, and also founded a school for Native Americans in Nevada.

Winner, South Dakota.   There was some dispute as to where a town would be established along the railroad right-of-way. This spot was the winner, thus giving rise to its unusual name.

Winona, Minnesota, was founded in 1851 and named for Winona, a prominent Dakota woman who was active during the forced removal of the Winnebagos from Iowa to Minnesota. The name *Winona,* which means "firstborn," was also popularized by an 1881 poem by H. L. Gordon called "Winona."

Winston-Salem, North Carolina, was created in 1913 out of two towns. Winston was founded in 1849 and named for Major Joseph Winston, a Revolutionary War soldier. Salem was settled by Moravians in 1776, who chose the name *Salem,* the old Hebrew word for "peace." Originally, these two small towns were only a mile apart.

Wiscasset, Maine, derives its name from an Abenaki term meaning "at the hidden outlet." It was a common practice for Native Americans to give a name to the place where a lake empties into a river, whereas Europeans generally named the lake and the river, but not the outlet.

Woburn, Massachusetts, was founded in 1642 and named for Woburn, England.

Woodbury, New Jersey, was settled by Quakers around 1633 and named for Quaker leader John Wood.

Woodland, California, was founded in 1853 by Henry Wyckoff, who named it for its location in a grove of oak trees.

Woonsocket, Rhode Island, began in 1666 when Richard Arnold built a sawmill on the Blackstone River. The name comes from *woonsocket,* a Native American term meaning "at the very steep hill" or possibly "thunder mist," alluding to a nearby waterfall.

Wooster, Ohio, was laid out in 1808 and named for General David Wooster, a Revolutionary War soldier. The Christmas tree was introduced to America here.

Worcester, Massachusetts. In 1673, settlers from eastern Massachusetts founded the village of Quinsigamond on what is now the site of Worcester. In 1684, King Charles II canceled the charter of the Massachusetts Bay Colony, which so angered the people of Quinsigamond that they renamed their village Worcester. They chose this name in recognition of the Battle of Worcester, in which Charles II suffered a great defeat during the English Civil War in 1651.

Wyandotte, Michigan, was settled in 1820 and named for the Wyandot, whose name is believed to mean "islanders" or "peninsula dwellers." This tribe, also known as the Huron, moved from Ontario to Michigan in 1730.

Yakima, Washington, was incorporated in 1886 and named for the Yakima, a Shahaptian tribe, whose name means "runaway" or "refugee." In 1855, the U.S. government grouped several tribes under the name Yakima, convinced them to cede their lands to the United States, and moved them to a reservation southwest of the town.

Yankton, South Dakota, derives its name from the Dakota term *ihanktonwane,* meaning "end village."

Yoncalla, Oregon,   derives its name from an Athapaskan term meaning "eagle."

Yonkers, New York,   was acquired from the Native American Wapinger confederacy by the Dutch West Indies Company in 1639. Dutch nobleman Jonkheer Adriaen Van der Donck, whose title *Jonkheer* means "young lord," was awarded a land grant here in 1646. Yonkers took its name from him.

York, Maine,   was settled in 1624 and named for James, duke of York and Albany. It was the first English city to be built on the American continent.

York, Pennsylvania,   was laid out in 1741 and named either for James, duke of York, or for York, England. It was the first European settlement in Pennsylvania.

Youngstown, Ohio,   was organized in 1802 and named for John Young, a surveyor from New York who purchased the land from the Connecticut Land Company in 1797. The city was incorporated in 1848.

Yuma, Arizona,   was laid out in 1854 and named Colorado City. Later it was named Arizona City, then renamed after the Yuma. The name derives from *yamayo*, a Native American title meaning "son of the captain," which was mistakenly applied to the entire tribe.

Zanesville, Ohio,   was founded in 1797 by Ebenezer Zane, who was given the land by congress so he could clear a road through the forest to Limestone, now Maysville, Kentucky. The road was called Zane's Trace. The popular Wild West author, Zane Grey (1875–1939), a descendant of Ebenezer Zane, was born here.

PART II

All Over the World

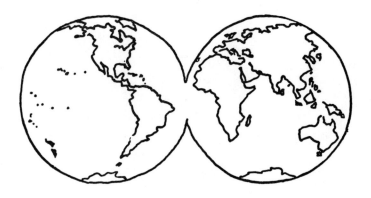

3

Nations

Afghanistan is from the Urdu word *stan*, "district," and Afghan, a tribe originally ruled by chief Malik Afghana.

Albania comes from the Latin *albus*, "white," and means "white land." The country is mountainous and often covered with snow. The country's name for itself is *Shqipëria*, which means "land of the eagle." The eagle has figured in the symbols of the rulers of Albania since the area was part of the Byzantine Empire.

Algeria derives its name from the ancient Arabic city Al Djazair, meaning uncertain. The English name for the city is Algiers, from which the country got its name.

Angola derives from the Bantu name for the region, Ngola, which Portuguese explorers could only pronounce by adding a syllable to the beginning.

Argentina derives from the Latin word *argentum*, which means "silver." The early European explorers found an abundance of silver there, which they compelled the indigenous people to mine for them. Native Americans were worked in a merciless fashion, so much so that four out of five died within a year after going underground. But they brought out silver by the ton. The town of Potosí, which is now in Bolivia, grew so rapidly that before long it became the largest city in the New World.

Armenia derives its name from the Aryan term *harminni*, meaning "mountains of Minya."

Australia derives from the old Latin name *Terra Australis*, meaning "southern land." This name originally referred to unknown lands south of the equator which the Greeks theorized must exist.

Austria comes from the Anglo-Saxon *Östreich*, which means "eastern kingdom."

Azerbaijan. This name derives from the Persian words *azer*, "fire," and *baijan*, "keeper." Azerbaijan is one of the former Soviet republics.

The Bahamas derives from the Native American *Guanahani*, meaning unknown, which the Spanish invaders badly distorted.

Bahrain comes from the Arabic word *bahar*, meaning "sea" or "lake." The full name means "two seas." Bahrain is made up of several islands in the Persian Gulf.

Bangladesh means "land of the Bengal." Bangladesh was once the eastern part of the Bengal province of the British Empire.

Barbados. Located off the northeast coast of South America, the name Barbados means "bearded." This name was given to the land by the early Portuguese because they saw so many beardlike vines on its trees.

Belgium comes from the name of an ancient European tribe, the Belgae. The Latin name *Belgium* means "land of the Belgae." In the Gallic Wars when Julius Caesar fought against these people in 58 B.C.E., it is said he found them to be the bravest of any he had ever fought.

Belize, formerly British Honduras, is named after its main town, which in the early days of European colonization grew up around a beacon used to guide ships at night. The town was named Belize after the old French word *belice*, meaning "beacon." Some, however, believe the name derives from the Scottish adventurer James Wallis, who founded a settlement there in 1610. Belize is a Spanish variant of Wallis.

Benin, formerly Dahomey, takes its name from the Latin word *benignus*, meaning "blessed."

Bhutan is bordered on the north by Tibet and on the south by India. In the local language, Tibet is called *Bhot*, and *atan* means "end," the whole name meaning "at the end of Tibet." The dragon is the national symbol of Bhutan, and the country is often called the Land of the Dragon.

Bolivia was named for Simon Bolivar (1783–1830), the South American patriot who liberated the people from Spanish rule. He was a great soldier, statesman, and liberator. He not only helped to liberate Bolivia, but also Colombia, Ecuador, Peru, and Venezuela.

Bosnia-Herzegovina. Once part of Yugoslavia, this nation is made up of two republics. Bosnia means "land of the River Bosna," and Herzegovina derives from a Teutonic name meaning "duchy of Herzog."

Botswana. The people of the country call themselves Batswana; their language is Tswana.

Brazil takes its name from *brasil*, which comes from the Portuguese word *braza*, meaning "burnt wood" or "live coal." The *braza* was a pigment-yielding wood used to make dye, a valuable product. Purple dye had been made in the Old World since 1000 B.C.E. The Egyptians knew how to make indigo, but after the fall of the Roman Empire this art had been neglected. With this new find in Brazil, the industry was made to thrive again. The land came to be known as *Terra de Brasil*, "land of the red-dye wood."

Bulgaria means "land of the Bulgars." The Bulgar tribe settled in the area in 681. Their name may derive from the same source as the name of the Volga River. The Bulgars migrated from the area of the Volga River.

Burma. See *Myanmar*.

Byelorus, or Belorus, was formerly part of the Soviet Union. Its name comes from the Russian words *byel*, "white, and *Rus*, "Russia." It is called White Russia because of the strong use of white in the national costume.

Cameroon, a republic in West Africa, became independent in 1960. The name derives from the Portuguese word *camarões*, meaning "prawns" or "shrimps." The name was applied by Portuguese explorers to what is now the Wouri River when they discovered shrimp there.

Canada. It is thought that Jacques Cartier, the French navigator who discovered the St. Lawrence River, gave Canada its name. The story is told of how he spent the winter in a Native American village near the site of present-day Quebec. One day when he was talking with a Native chief, the chief waved his arms toward the east and exclaimed, *"Kannahta!"* Cartier thought he was referring to the entire country, but actually the chief was trying to tell him there was a nearby Native village. The Wyandot word *kannahta* means "village" or "collection of lodges." No matter, thereafter Cartier referred to the whole land as Kanata, from which the name Canada came.

Cape Verde. Formerly ruled by the Portuguese, this group of fifteen islands off the coast of West Africa got its independence in 1975. Cape Verde, in Portuguese, means "green cape."

Central African Republic became independent of French colonial rule in 1960, whereupon it changed its named from Central African Empire. The name is descriptive of the country's location.

Chad. An independent state in equatorial Africa, it gets its name from Lake Chad, a large, shallow lake on its southeastern border. The name Chad derives from the indigenous name *ssaghi* or *tsade*, meaning "water."

Chile　is the southernmost country of South America. The longest and narrowest country in the world, it runs three thousand miles long along the continent's western edge. It starts far north in the nitrate desert and terminates in the polar seas to the extreme south. Nowhere is it more than two hundred miles wide, and that width includes the snow-capped peaks of the Andes Mountains. Its name comes from the indigenous Aymara word *tshili*, meaning "snow."

China　took its name from the first emperor of the Tshin Dynasty in the third century B.C.E.

Colombia　was named for Christopher Columbus.

Congo,　formerly a French colony, derives its name from the Mandingo word *kong*, meaning "mountains." Kongo was an ancient kingdom which flourished there long before Europeans invaded the nation. Today about half the population are members of the Kongo tribe. The name was also used by the Belgians for their own colony, Belgian Congo, now Zaire.

Costa Rica　is Spanish for "rich coast." Christopher Columbus gave it this name on his fourth voyage to the New World, but the early explorers did not find the riches there that they expected.

Croatia　means "land of the Croats." The name Croat is derived from a Slavic tribe, Hrvati, which means "people of the hills," and which other Europeans pronounced "cravat" and the English changed to Croat. Croatia is one of the former republics of Yugoslavia.

Cuba　took its name from the indigenous name *Cuban-acan*, meaning "center place." When Columbus landed here in 1492, the word *cuba* was used in many place names on the island; it means "place."

Cyprus. The Greek name for the island was Kypros, which came from the Greek word *cuprum*, meaning "copper." A lot of copper has been mined in Cyprus from earliest times.

Czech Republic. This country is named after its principal tribe, the Czechs. Two Czech regions, Bohemia and Moravia, were combined with Slovakia after World War I and called Czechoslovakia. In 1992, Czechoslovakia split into two nations, the Czech Republic and Slovakia.

Denmark derives from a tribe of people known as Danes; the name means "plain of the Danes."

Dominica was named by Christopher Columbus; it was discovered on *Dies Dominica*, Spanish for "the Lord's day," Sunday.

Dominican Republic occupies about two-thirds of the island of Hispaniola. Columbus named a European settlement on the island Santo Domingo after Saint Dominic, his father's patron saint.

Ecuador is astride the equator, from which it gets its name. The name was first applied by Simon Bolivar (1783–1830), the liberator of the northern republics of South America. In 1824, he divided his Republic of Gran Colombia into districts and departments and decreed that the northernmost department of the Quito district be known as Ecuador. Six years later, the people of Quito broke free from Gran Colombia, and the República del Ecuador was the name agreed upon by their first constitutional assembly.

Egypt   derives from the Greek word *Aigyptos*, which was derived from the Babylonian name for Menes, the first Pharaoh to unite the northern and southern kingdoms of the Nile.

El Salvador   derives its name from its capital, San Salvador, meaning "holy savior." Columbus gave the city that name in honor of Christ the Savior.

England.   See *United Kingdom*.

Eritrea   is named after the Erythraean Sea, which derives its name from the Greek word *erythros*, meaning "red." The English name for the Erythraean is the Red Sea.

Estonia   was formerly part of the Soviet Union. Its name derives from a tribe of people called the Est, or Latinized, Estonian.

Ethiopia   is a Greek name, from *aitho*, "burn" and *ops*, "face." It means "land of the people with sunburned faces."

Finland   derives from an early group of people living there who called themselves Finns. It means "land of the Finns."

France.   In the fifth century, several tribes from central Europe—Vandals, Goths, Franks, Alamans, and Burgundians—established themselves in what is now France. Of these tribes, the Franks, whose name is believed to have come from the *franca*, a kind of javelin, were destined to have the greatest influence on the country's future. Before the end of the century, the rough and rugged Franks had conquered almost all of Gaul and created a fairly unified state. It was from the Franks that France took its name.

French Guiana   is an overseas department of France. It is located in the Guiana region of South America.

Gabon   derives from the Portuguese word *gabon*, meaning "cabin." Early Portuguese explorers, for reasons which are not clear, gave that name to a river in West Africa.

The Gambia,   a republic of West Africa, was named for the Gambia River, one of Africa's finest waterways. The indigenous name *Gambre*, meaning "river," was corrupted to Gambia when the Portuguese invaded the area. The country became independent in 1965.

Georgia   was formerly part of the Soviet Union. It derives its name from the Greek word *georgos*, meaning "farmer." The region supports a great deal of agriculture.

Germany   derives from the large group of Indo-European (or possibly Celtic) tribes called the *Germani*, meaning "hill dwellers." The Germans call their country *Deutschland* (pronounced "DOICH-lahnt"), which, in old German, means "land of the people." The German settlers in Pennsylvania are known as Pennsylvania Dutch due to the mispronunciation of the term *Deutsch*.

Ghana is the name of an ancient kingdom; its meaning is unknown. Other versions of the name are Ginnie or Juinie, the origin of the name Guinea.

Granada was named in 1498 after a province of Spain.

Great Britain. See *United Kingdom*

Greece is a name derived from *Graikoi*, the name of a small tribe from what is now Greece. The Roman name for them was *Graeci*, and this name came to be applied to all the people of the country. The Greeks call their country Ellas.

Guatemala derives from the Native word *quauhtemallan*, which means either "land of trees" or "land of the eagle." There is also the possibility the name came from the word *guhatezmalike*, meaning "volcano of water."

Guinea, formally called the Republic of Guinea, is an ancient name of uncertain meaning which was used throughout the coastal areas of West Africa. One translation is "land of many rivers." There are two other Guineas in Africa: Equatorial Guinea and Guinea-Bissau (formerly Portuguese Guinea). Papua New Guinea, made up of several islands in the Pacific, is an independent member of the British Commonwealth.

Guinea-Bissau is an independent nation bordering on the Republic of Guinea. It is called Guinea-Bissau, for its capital city Bissau, to differentiate it from the Republic of Guinea.

Guyana, formerly British Guiana, is the largest of three countries in the Guiana region of South America. Guyana derives from *Guaya-na*, a tribal name meaning "we, the esteemed," although some believe it means "wild coast." The other two countries in the region are Suriname (formerly Dutch Guiana), and French Guiana.

Haiti is an indigenous word meaning "craggy" or "rough," referring to the mountainous land.

Honduras, a Central American country, was first visited by Columbus in 1502. His sailors gave Honduras its name because they had difficulty finding shallow water for anchoring ships off the shore. The name means "deep water" in Spanish.

Hong Kong derives its name from the Chinese words *hong*, "fragrant," and *kong*, "harbor." The name refers to the incense trade which was important to the development of the port. Hong Kong became a British colony in 1942, and is scheduled to become part of China in 1997.

Hungary derives its name from that of the Hun tribe, who under Attila the Hun conquered the area in 450 C.E. However, in 870, the Magyar tribe took the area, and have remained there to the present time. The Hungarian name for their country is Magyarország.

Iceland means "land of ice." The name derives from the Icelandic name, which is pronounced "ice-land" but spelled Island. However, the whole island is not as cold as the name suggests. The southern coastal region is bathed by a warm ocean current, which makes the temperature mild. Long ago, volcanoes covered the island and left the soil fertile. About one-third of the population of Iceland are farmers. The vegetables are irrigated with water from warm springs on the island. In some places, the Icelanders pipe water from the hot springs to heat their homes and public buildings.

India   derives its name from the Indus River, the great river which flows through India, Pakistan, and China. The Indus got its name from the ancient Sanskrit word *sindhu*, meaning "river."

Indonesia   is a Greek term meaning "islands of the Indies." The name was applied to it in 1949 when Indonesia gained independence from Dutch rule.

Iran   is an ancient Persian name for the kingdom of Babylonia. The Aryans, an ancient Indo-European tribe, derive their name from Iran.

Iraq   derives from the ancient Persian name for the kingdom of Babylonia, Iran. Iraq is a later dialect. However, some say the name comes from an Arabic word meaning "origins." Iraq was formed from three Turkish provinces at the end of World War I in an old country that was called *Mesopotamia*, Greek for "between two rivers." This land was the home of what many believe to be the oldest civilization in the western hemisphere.

Ireland   comes from the word Eire (pronounced "air"), the Gaelic name for the country. Its poetic name Erin also derives from Eire.

Israel   derives from the ancient Hebrew phrase *yish-ra-el*, meaning "people of God." Israel was created as a Jewish homeland in 1947 by the partition of Palestine.

Italy   derives from the Latin name *Italia*, which meant "land of the calf." The area was rich in cattle in pre-Roman days.

Ivory Coast   derives from the French name *Côte d'Ivoire*, "Coast of Ivory." The French began to trade in West African ivory in 1842. When the country became independent in 1960, the name was retained.

Jamaica   derives its name from *Xaymaca*, an Arawak name meaning "land of wood and water." Columbus named the island Santiago (St. James) in 1494. When the British renamed it in 1655, they took the Arawak name but spelled it Jamaica, evoking the name James.

Japan.   In ancient times, the Japanese called their land Yamato, but when they started to deal with China, they described their country with two Chinese characters meaning "source of the sun," to indicate their location east of China. The two characters in the Chinese language were pronounced "jih-pen," which is the origin of the name Japan.

Jordan   is named for the Jordan River, which forms part of its western boundary.

Kampuchea.   The European name for this country is Cambodia. The name derives from Kambu, the legendary founder of the Khmer, or Cambodian people. It is the smallest country in Indochina.

Kazakhstan, formerly part of the Soviet Union, is a Turkic name meaning "district of the Kazakhs." The Kazakh tribe, whose name means "riders," gave it its name.

Kenya lies on the equator in eastern Africa. It was named after Mount Kenya.

Kirghizia was formerly part of the Soviet Union. Its inhabitants call themselves *Kirghiz*, a Persian name meaning "desert rangers," from which the country takes its name.

Korea derives from the Koryu dynasty, who came into power in 918 C.E. Marco Polo brought the name Korea to Europe in the thirteenth century. The Koreans called their peninsula *Cho-son*, often spelled *Chosen*, which means "land of the morning calm." Its history, however, has not been calm. It has been a battleground where strong neighboring countries have overrun the land in an attempt to gain control of it.

Kuwait is bordered on the north and west by Iraq, on the south by Saudi Arabia, and on the east by the Persian Gulf. The name comes from an Arabic word meaning "little fort."

Laos is a mountainous, landlocked country in Southeast Asia. About half of the country's four million people belong to a group called Lao, which is also the official language. Hence its name. Laos became a center of world attention in the 1960s when fighting broke out between the communist and non-communist factions.

Latvia was formerly part of the Soviet Union. The people who live there are called Lett. Latvia is a distortion of their own tribal name Lietuva, also the source of the name Lithuania. The Letts occupy the northern part of the Lietuva region.

Lebanon, derives its name from *Gebel Libnan*, or Lebanon Mountain, which comes from the Arabic words for "mountain" and "white." Lebanon Mountain is covered with snow most of the year.

Lesotho was called Basutoland by British colonists, after the African citizens who called themselves Basotho (pronounced "ba-SOO-too"). The name Lesotho ("le-SOO-too") came from this. The country got its independence from Great Britain in 1966. Its population is about 1,711,000. Lesotho is completely surrounded by South Africa.

Liberia is a Latin term meaning "country of the free." It was founded in 1847 on the coast of West Africa by former African-American slaves.

Libya is an ancient Greek name of unknown origin. At one time the name was applied to the entire continent of Africa.

Liechtenstein was named for the House of Liechtenstein, an Austrian noble family which was assigned the principality in 1719.

Lithuania was formerly part of the Soviet Union. The name comes from a distortion of the local tribal name Lietuva, also the source of the name Latvia. The Lithuanians occupy the southern part of the Lietuva region.

Luxembourg   had its beginning when Count Siegfried of Ardennes built a castle there in 963. The Teutonic name for the castle was *Lutzelburg*, meaning "little fortress."

Macau   was founded by the Portuguese in 1557, when the Chinese granted permission to establish a trading post on the site. Built on the site of the ancient Chinese temple Ma Kok, dedicated to the goddess Ama, this small nation consists of a section of the mainland and two nearby islands. The early Chinese name was *Ama Ngao*, meaning "Ama bay," which was shortened to Amacao, then Macau.

Malagasy Republic,   formerly known as Madagascar, is the fourth largest island in the world. It lies 250 miles east of the African coast, and it is almost as large as Texas. It was named the Malagasy Republic because nearly 98 percent of the people are Malay, and their name for themselves is Malagasy. The name Madagascar was a European distortion of that name.

Malawi   means "flaming waters." The name refers to the reflections of the sun in the surface of Lake Nyasa.

Malaysia,   located in Southeast Asia, was named for the Malay people who settled there in 100 C.E. The name *Malay* means "people of the mountains."

Maldives   derives its name from the Sanskrit words *diva*, "island," and *mal*, "thousand," and means "a thousand islands." In fact, the country is made up of some two thousand islands.

Mali   is a landlocked republic in West Africa. France colonized the area and called it French Sudan. When it gained independence in 1960, it chose the name Mali, the ancient name of their powerful empire. *Mali* is the indigenous word meaning "hippopotamus," a symbol of power and strength.

Malta   derives from the Phoenician word *melita*, meaning "refuge."

Mauritania   derives from the Greek word *mauros*, meaning "dark," which referred to the mysterious land of which the Greeks knew little. The Romans called the northwest part of the African continent *Mauretania*, meaning "land of the dark." Mauritania, with a slight change in spelling, was colonized by the French and gained its independence in 1960.

Mauritius   is an independent island in the Indian Ocean. The Dutch claimed it in 1596 and named it for Prince Maurice of Nassau-Orange, son of King William of the Netherlands.

Mexico   is a Latin American republic that borders the United States in the southwest. The country's name came from the Aztec people who lived where Mexico now stands. Mexitel is the ancient Aztec war god, and *co* is the Aztec word for "place." The name Mexico was given to the "place of the war god."

Moldavia   was formerly part of the Soviet Union. It is believed to derive from a tribal name, but its meaning is both ancient and obscure.

Monaco derives from the ancient Greek name for a Phoenician temple, *Heracles Monoikos*, meaning "Hercules One-House." It was given this name because there was only one temple in the area, and it was dedicated to Hercules. This country has no income taxes and no unemployment. Since it is completely surrounded by France, French is the language there.

Mongolia derives from the Mongols, who in the thirteenth century built the largest land empire in history, extending from Eastern Asia to Western Europe. Mongolia is an autonomous region of China.

Montenegro along with Serbia, is one of the last remaining republics of Yugoslavia. The name, meaning "black mountains," is derived from the Italian words *monte*, "mount," and *negro*, "black." The local hills are covered by dense pine woods which appear to be black.

Morocco derives its name from a corruption of Marrakech, the name of its capital city. However, some believe the name means "country of the Moors."

Mozambique comes from a Portuguese distortion of the indigenous name *Ma-sam-buco*, meaning "the boats," which refers to the harbor.

Myanmar also known as Burma, derives from the Chinese words *mian* or *mien*, meaning "strong," and the suffix *-ma*, meaning "honorable." Burma is an English corruption of Mianma, the country's correct name.

Namibia is located on the Atlantic coast of southern Africa. The nation was ruled by South Africa as a territory until 1993. Its name is taken from the Namib Desert.

Nepal is located between India and the Tibetan region of China. It took its name from the Nepal Valley.

The Netherlands comes from the Dutch word *neder*, meaning "lower." The name refers to the fact that much of the Netherlands is below sea level. Half of the country would be flooded if there were no dikes to keep out the water. For centuries, the Dutch have been fighting the sea, pushing its waters back, claiming more and more of the land.

Sometimes the Netherlands is referred to as Holland, but this name originally designated only one province. The Netherlands is the official name for this artificially created country.

Amsterdam, Rotterdam, Edam, and other cities of the Netherlands ending in *dam* signify that their growth has been made possible because of the building of dikes.

New Zealand. In 1642, Abel Janszoon Tasman, a sea captain working for the Dutch East India Company, became the first European to sight New Zealand. The Dutch company kept Tasman's discovery a secret in order to prevent its rival, the British East India Company, from taking over the island. The Dutch named the island *Nieuw Zeeland*, "new Zeeland," after Tasman's home province in the Netherlands. *Zeeland* means "sea land," and the Dutch province is composed of several low-lying sea islands. The New Zealand spelling, with an "e" changed to an "a," is meant to distinguish New Zealand from its Dutch namesake.

Nicaragua   is the largest country in Central America. Its name comes from that of a Native chief, Nicarac, who lived in the land when the Spaniards conquered it in the 1500s.

Niger and **Nigeria**   took their names from the Niger River, which derives its name from the Berber word *n'ghirren,* meaning "river." *Niger* is also a Latin word meaning "black," which some believe to be the source of the name.

Norway   comes from the old Scandinavian name *Nor-eike,* meaning "north kingdom." Norway occupies the northernmost part of the Scandinavian peninsula.

Pakistan   comes from the Urdu words *pakh,* "pure," and *stan,* "district." Pakistan was created as a Muslim homeland out of five provinces of India when the predominantly Hindu nation gained its independence in 1947. Muslims assign meaningful symbolism to the name. The name evokes the Punjab, Afghan, Kashmir, and Sindh provinces by their initials, and ends in the word *stan,* representing Baluchistan.

Palestine   means "land of the Philistines" or, as it is sometimes translated, "land of the strangers." In 1947, Palestine was partitioned by the United Nations into Arab and Jewish homelands, and no longer exists as an independent nation.

Panama,   founded in 1903, is the youngest republic in the western hemisphere. The name comes from a Guarani word meaning "butterfly." A thriving city named Panama was recorded here in 1518, and it soon lent its name to the isthmus, the gulf, and the country.

Papua New Guinea. The Spanish explorer Ynigo Ortiz de Retez landed on this island in 1546 and called it New Guinea, the inhabitants looking much the same to him as the Africans of Guinea. The name Papua, derived from the Malay word *papuwah*, meaning "woolly," was used by Malaysian sailors to refer to the woolly-haired Melanesian inhabitants. Later, among the indigenous citizens, Papua became an accepted name. However, the country was officially called New Guinea until it gained independence in 1975, when Papua was added to the name.

Paraguay derives from the Guarani words *para*, "water" or "river," and *guay*, "place." The Paraguay River is the fifth largest river in South America.

Peru derives its name from the Quechua word *piru*, meaning "an abundance of land."

Philippines. The Philippines, an island country in the southwest Pacific Ocean, was given its name in 1543, when a Spanish admiral visited the islands and named them in honor of the prince who became King Philip II of Spain (1527–1598).

Poland is a country of plains and gently rolling hills in central Europe. Its name derives from an old Slavic word meaning "level land." The tribe who lived there were called Polians or Poles.

Portugal is the westernmost country of continental Europe. From the early days of history, there was a port at the mouth of the Douro River, in the northern part of Portugal, called Portus-cale. The Latin *portus* means "port" or "haven," and the ancient term *cale* means "port" or "harbor." In time, the name became Portucale, which was the origin of the name Portugal.

Puerto Rico is a Spanish name meaning "rich port." In 1508, Juan Ponce de León (1460–1521) was commissioned by the king of Spain to settle the island. He founded a village near San Juan Bay, which he named Puerto Rico, possibly to encourage settlement. The name later came to be applied to the whole island. Today, Puerto Rico is a U.S. territory.

Rhodesia was a colonial country; it no longer appears on the map of Africa. It was named for Cecil Rhodes (1853–1902), a British businessman who began exploiting the area in 1889. It later split into Northern Rhodesia (now Zambia) and Southern Rhodesia (now Zimbabwe).

Romania derives from the Latinized version of the Turkish name *Rumeli*, which means "land of the Romans."

Russia was the largest republic of the Union of Soviet Socialist Republics (U.S.S.R.), which ceased to be a union in 1989. The name derives from the Rus, an ancient Scandinavian tribe led by Chief Rourik. The Russian word *soviet* means "council." The seat of government was called the *Kremlin*, which means "fortress."

San Marino, the smallest republic in Europe, covers only thirty-seven square miles. According to legend, it was founded in the third century by Marinus, a Christian stonemason from Dalmatia, as a refuge from religious persecution. Marinus became the patron saint of the republic, which took its name from him.

Saudi Arabia. The Muslim leader Abd al-Aziz ibn Saud named the country after himself in 1932. The name means "land of the Arabs of Saud."

Scotland. See *United Kingdom.*

Senegal, in West Africa, took its name from the Senegal River, which forms its northern border with Mauritania. Senegal is a corruption of Azanague, a Berber tribal name which the Portuguese pronounced "Senaga" and used for the river name. Senegal became independent in 1960.

Serbia means "land of the Serbs." One of the remaining republics of Yugoslavia, this country may have gotten its name from the Greek word *serbos,* meaning "slave," but this is uncertain.

Seychelles, an independent island nation far off the east coast of Africa, derives it name from Morau de Seychelles, finance minister of King Louis XV of France. The British conquered this French colony in 1794 but retained the French name. Seychelles gained independence in 1976.

Sierra Leone is a Spanish name meaning "mountains of the lions." The name refers both to the animal and to the majestic and fierce attributes of the country's people.

Singapore is one of the greatest ports in the world. It gets its name from the Sanskrit words *singha*, "lion," and *pore*, "city." The name means "city of the lions."

Slovakia. This country is named after the Slavs, a large group of Indo-European tribes which today inhabit many nations. Until 1992, Slovakia was part of Czechoslovakia.

Slovenia, like Slovakia, is named after the Slavs. It is one of the former republics of Yugoslavia.

Somalia is an independent country in East Africa made up of areas formerly known as British Somaliland and Italian Somaliland. It got its name from the Somali tribes who arrived there in the thirteenth century.

South Africa is an independent country that occupies the southern tip of Africa. The Dutch gave South Africa its name when they colonized the area in 1652.

Spain derives from the ancient Romans, who called the area *Hispania*, a name possibly derived from an indigenous name. Both the current Spanish name *España* and the English name came from *Hispania*.

Sri Lanka was colonized by Britain, which named the island Ceylon. It gained its independence in 1948, and in 1972 renamed itself Sri Lanka. The title *Sri* (pronounced "shree") in the Sinhala language means "glorious," "resplendent," or "venerable." The full name of the island means "glorious land."

Sudan was called Kush as early as 1500 B.C.E. *Sudan* is an Arabic word meaning "black."

Suriname, formerly Dutch Guiana (or Netherlands Guiana), derives its name from the Surinam River. It took its present name in 1948.

Swaziland, in southern Africa, took its name from the Swazi tribes who have lived in the area since the sixteenth century.

Sweden derives from the ancient Scandinavian name *Sviarika*, meaning "kingdom of the Svears." The Svears were one of the earliest tribes to live in the area.

Switzerland derives from the medieval canton (province) of Schwyz. Switzerland was created in 1291 by a confederation of peacefully united cantons. The Latin name for the country is *Helvetia*, which is often used in place of the four different names of Switzerland in its four official languages.

Syria derives its name from that of the ancient region of Suri. Suri is a Semitic name of unknown meaning.

Tadzhikistan, or Tajikistan, is a Turkic name meaning "district of the Tadzhiks." The country was formerly part of the Soviet Union.

Taiwan, on the island of Formosa, is a Chinese name meaning "terraced bay." The mountain slopes of the island have been terraced to provide level surfaces for housing and agriculture.

Tanganyika, formerly Tanzania, derives its name from that of Lake Tanganyika. The Bantu name derives from *tanganya*, "to gather," and *nyika*, the name of a local water chestnut, and refers to the great masses of such plants on the water.

Thailand. In the Thai language, *tai* means "free." Coupled with the English suffix *-land*, the name means "land of the free." Thailand is one of the few Asian nations which has never been under colonial domination. The country was formerly known as Siam; the named was changed to Thailand in 1939.

Tibet derives its name from the Mongolian name *Bod*, meaning simply "the country," which was corrupted by Arabs, and later by Europeans, into its present form. Tibet is an autonomous region of China.

Trinidad and Tobago. This nation is composed of Caribbean islands. The island of Trinidad was named in 1498 by Christopher Columbus, due to the fact that is resembles three small islands. The name means "three" or "trinity." The origin of Tobago is in dispute. Some say it was named by Columbus, who thought the island resembled the *tobaco,* or inhaling tube, used by the indigenous people. Others believe the name derives from the Spanish word *trabajo,* "troubles," referring to perilous journeys undertaken there by Spanish explorers in 1500.

Tunisia. The history of Tunis, its capital, is lost in antiquity. It is mentioned in Greek and Latin texts under the name *Tynes,* or *Tunes.* The nation took its name from its capital city.

Turkey derives its name from that of the Turkish tribes that invaded what is now known as Turkey. The name *Turk* means "strong." The Ottoman Empire, whose name came from a legendary Turkish leader named Othman, came to an end in 1922, and Turkey became a republic in 1923.

Uganda is named after the Ganda, a tribe which in the nineteenth century had established a powerful empire in the area. The Bantu prefix *u-* means "land of."

Ukraine is a Slavic word meaning "frontier" or "boundary." It was formerly part of the Soviet Union.

Union of Soviet Socialist Republics. See *Russia*.

United Arab Emirates was created in 1971 by the union of seven Arab emirates: Abu Dhabi, Ajman, Al Fujayrah, Ash Shariqah, Dubai, Ra's al Khaymah, and Umm al Qaywayn. An emirate is a country ruled by an emir.

The United Kingdom of Great Britain and Northern Ireland is composed of England, Scotland, Wales, and part of Ireland. The first three nations cover the Isle of Britain, and are therefore known as **Great Britain**. When England annexed Northern Ireland, that name was added to its title.

A tribe known as the Britons inhabited the island and from their name came the word Britain. **England** was named for the Angles, an early Germanic (Saxon) tribe that invaded the country and settled there. The name **Wales** comes from the Saxon language and means "strangers." The Latin name for Wales is *Cambria*, which comes from the Welsh name *Cymru*, meaning "fellow natives." **Ireland** comes from the word *Eire*, the Gaelic name for the country. Ireland's poetic name,

Erin, also derives from *Eire*. A Celtic tribe called the Scots migrated from Ireland to northern Britain in the sixth century and settled on the coast, giving **Scotland** its name.

The United States of America was originally formed out of thirteen British colonies who declared their independence in 1776. The name United States was chosen to indicate the independent and united status of the thirteen members, no longer colonies. The name America is derived from the name given to the northern and southern continents of the New World.

Uruguay took its name from the Uruguay River. *Uruguay* is a Guarani word meaning "bird's tail," and refers to the fanlike appearance of a waterfall in the river.

Uzbekistan is a Turkic name which means "district of the Uzbeks." The tribal name Uzbek derives from Uzbeg Khan, a descendant of Genghis Khan. The republic was formerly part of the Soviet Union.

Vatican City was named for the principal residence of the Pope, the Vatican Palace. The palace derives its name from the Latin word *vaticinatio*, meaning "prophesy."

Venezuela is a republic on the northern coast of South America. *Venezuela* is a Spanish word meaning "little Venice." When Spanish explorers reached the country, they found an indigenous village built on wooden poles above the shallow waters of Lake Maracaibo. The village reminded them of Venice, Italy, and they named it Venezuela. Later this name came to be applied to the whole country.

Vietnam is a Chinese name meaning "far south." The country is indeed far south of China.

Wales. See *United Kingdom.*

Yemen derives from an Arabic term meaning "to the south" or "to the right." Yemen is located on the southern end of the Arabic Peninsula.

Yugoslavia was pieced together out of six small Slavic nations after World War I: Bosnia-Herzegovina, Croatia, Macedonia, Montenegro, Serbia, and Slovenia. The name comes from the Slavic word *yug,* "south," and means "land of the southern Slavs." In 1991, Yugoslavia disintegrated as several republics became independent once again; only Serbia and Montenegro remain.

Zaire, formerly Belgian Congo, took its present name in 1971. The name Zaire is an ancient one derived from a local language. It means simply "river," and the name was adopted by early Portuguese explorers who named the main waterway the Zaire River. The area was colonized by Belgium in the 1880s. The Belgians named the area Belgian Congo and called the river the Congo River. The river was renamed Zaire in 1971 when the country was renamed.

Zambia, formerly Northern Rhodesia, became independent of colonial rule in 1964. It took its name from the Zambezi River, which derives its name from the Bantu words *zam,* "great," and *bezi,* "water."

Zimbabwe, formerly Southern Rhodesia, gained independence in 1980. The name Zimbabwe means "dwelling place of a chief," referring to a great circular village where the local chief resides.

4

Cities and Provinces

Acapulco, Mexico, is believed to have gotten its name from an Aztec term meaning "destroyed" or "conquered."

Addis Ababa, Ethiopia, is an Arab name meaning "new flower."

Adelaide, South Australia, was named in honor of Queen Adelaide (1792–1849), wife of King William IV of England.

Apple River, Nova Scotia, Canada. This seaside town is said to have gotten its name when a ship laden with apples was wrecked in the neighborhood more than one hundred years ago.

Alberta, Canada (province), was named for Princess Louise Caroline Alberta (1848–1939), daughter of Queen Victoria and husband of the governor-general of Canada.

Alexandria, Egypt, was founded in 332 B.C.E. at the mouth of the Nile River by Alexander the Great, who named it for himself. Alexander was born on one continent, lived on another, and died on a third. He is buried at Alexandria. Although Alexander died before the city was finished, the Ptolemies, who became rulers of Egypt, carried out his plans. Alexander named many cities for himself. He hoped that this city would become the central city of the world.

Allahabad, India,   is an Arab name meaning "city of God."

Amsterdam, Netherlands,   was originally named Amstelredamme, "Amstel's dam," referring to a nearby river dam built in 1240 by Giesebrech van Amstel. The river is also named for Amstel.

Ankara, Turkey,   derives its name from the ancient Galatian city name *Ancyra*, meaning "valley."

Aqaba, Jordan.   This Arab name means "cliff" or "slope," referring to a steep hill west of the city.

Athens, Greece.   This city is believed to have been named for its patron, Athené, or Athena, the Greek goddess of wisdom.

Baden-Baden, Germany.   *Bad* is the German word for "bath," and it indicates the presence of mineral springs in the area. Since the time of the Roman empire, bathing in hot springs has been considered good for one's health. *Baden* means "at the baths," and at one time there were many towns with this name. This town came to be called *Baden-Baden*, meaning "Bath town in Bath duchy," to distinguish it from other Badens.

Baghdád, Iraq. Built in 763, this city's Persian name comes from the words *baga*, "god," and *dad*, "gift," meaning "gift of God."

Bangkok, Thailand, in the Thai language, means "water-flower village." This city's previous name was *Krung Thep*, meaning "city of angels."

Barcelona, Spain, founded in 237 B.C.E., was named for Hamilcar Barca, a Carthaginian military leader and father of the famous general Hannibal. The city was originally named Barcina. The Romans called it Barcinona, and it later came to be known as Barcelona. The name *Barca* means "lightning."

Beijing, China, means "northern capital." The city was named by the rulers of the Ming dynasty. At one time, China had two capitals; the southern capital was called Nanjing. Beijing was previously called Peking in English; this is an altered pronunciation of the name.

Belgrade, Serbia (Yugoslavia). This city's Slavic name is *Beograd*, meaning "white city."

Berlin, Germany. Many possible origins for the name of this city have been put forth, including the Wendish words *berle*, "uncultivated ground"; *barlin*, "shelter"; or *brljina*, "pool" or "pond."

Berne, Switzerland, took its name from the hometown of founder Berchtold of Zähringen, who came from Verona, Italy. The German name for Verona is Berne.

Bethlehem, Jordan, is a Hebrew name meaning "house of bread."

Brisbane, New South Wales, Australia, was named for the Brisbane River, which was named in honor of Scottish General Thomas Makdougall Brisbane, then governor of New South Wales.

Brussel, Belgium. In the sixth century, Saint Gary, bishop of Cambrai, founded a humble settlement on an island in the river Senne. His village was named *Bruocsella,* "city of the marshes," due to its location. Bruocsella, now called Bruxelles, was to become the largest and most beautiful city of Belgium, and it later gave its name to brussel sprouts. The city is often called Brussels, due to the pronunciation of the silent "s" on the city's Belgian name.

Buenos Aires, Argentina, was settled in 1536 by Spaniard Pedro de Mendoza, who named it *Santa Maria de los Buenos Aires,* "Saint Mary of fair winds." The name was later shortened.

Burgundy, France (historical province). The name Burgundy originated in the sixth century, when the Burgundians moved into Gaul (France) from Germany.

Cairo, Egypt. The name Cairo comes from the Arab *Al Qahirah,* "the victorious." Arabs conquered North Africa and built the city in 968, making it their capital.

Calcutta, India, was founded on the site of an ancient village in 1630. Its name comes from the Indian village name Kalikata, meaning unknown. Calcutta gave its name to calico cloth, which was first made there.

Calgary, Alberta, Canada. The Royal Canadian Mounted Police established a post here in 1875. The commander, Colonel James F. MacLeod (1836–1894) named it in honor of his ancestral home, Calgary, Scotland. *Calgary* is a Gaelic word meaning "clear, running water."

Cambridge, England. This city lies on a river which was once called Granta, a Celtic name of unknown origin. *Cam* is believed to be a corruption of *Granta*, and Cambridge is the modern version of the ancient village name Grantabridge, referring to a bridge over the river.

Canton, China, is the English version of the Chinese name Guanzhou. The meaning of the name is uncertain.

Casablanca, Morocco. This city takes its name from the Spanish words *casa*, "house," and *blanca*, "white." The city's official name is *Dar al Baida*, an Arab name also meaning "house of white."

Castile, Spain, derives its name from the Spanish word *castilo*, which means "castle."

Chapultepec, Mexico, is an Aztec name meaning "grasshopper hill."

Charlotte, Prince Edward Island, Canada, was named for Queen Charlotte (1744–1818), wife of King George III of England.

Colombo, Sri Lanka, is the capital of Sri Lanka. The city was originally known as *Kolamba*, an indigenous term meaning both "port" and "leafy mano tree." Portuguese traders heard the name in 1517 and immediately seized upon it for its resemblance to the name Columbus, which they spelled Colombo.

Colon, Panama. Americans who went to Panama to build a railroad founded the city in 1852 and named it Aspinwall after William H. Aspinwall, a railroad promoter. In 1890, the Panamanians renamed the city for Columbus. Colon is a Spanish form of Columbus.

Copenhagen, Denmark. Founded in approximately 1000, its earliest name was *Höfn*, meaning simply "haven" or "harbor." To distinguish it from other harbors, its name was later modified to *Kjømannshavn*, "merchant's harbor." Today the city is called Køenhavn. Copenhagen is an English version of the name.

Dublin, Ireland, derives its name from the Celtic words *dubh linne*, meaning "black pool." It is situated across the Irish Sea from Blackpool, England.

Dunkerque, France. Called Dunkirk in English, this town derives its name from a seventh-century name meaning "dune church." The beaches there are wide and sandy, and bridges connect the harbor to the town.

Edinburgh, Scotland. The name means "Edwin's city." Edwin was a seventh-century king of Northumbria, a northern region of Britain. *Burgh* is an Anglo-Saxon word for "city."

Edmonton, Alberta, Canada, was named after Fort Edmonton, established in 1795, which was named for the English city of Edmonton, hometown of the founder's clerk.

Fort Amador, Panama, was built in 1917 and named in honor of the first president of the Republic of Panama, Manuel Amador Guerreo. It is located on the eastern end of the Panama Canal.

Fort Frontenac, Ontario, Canada, was built in 1673 by Louis de Buade, comte de Frontenac (1620–1698), who was then governor of the French possessions of North America. It was later named in his honor.

Frankfurt-am-Main, Germany. This city's early name was Franconian Ford, because it was at a shallow ford on the River Main. *Franconian* meant "in the land of the Franks." Over time, the name was elided to Frankfurt, and now it is styled *Frankfurt-am-Main,* meaning "on the River Main."

Fredericton, New Brunswick, Canada, was named for Frederick, Prince of Wales (1707–1751), son of King George II of England. The British founded the city in 1762 on the site of an abandoned French settlement. It became the capital of New Brunswick in 1785.

Gaza, Israel, is three miles from the Mediterranean Sea and about fifty miles southwest of Jerusalem. It derives its name from an Arab word meaning "treasury." The town is located in the Gaza Strip, a partition of Israel. The thin, open cloth called gauze, named for Gaza, was first made here.

Gibraltar. This British colony occupies a rocky peninsula on the southern shores of Spain. Gibraltar was known to the early Mediterranean peoples as one of the two Pillars of Hercules; the other pillar stood across the Strait of Gibraltar on the African coast. In 711, Arab military leader Tariq ibn Zayid invaded the area and seized the mountain. The Arabs gave it the name *Gebel al Tariq*, "mountain of Tariq," which later developed into the name Gibraltar.

Glasgow, Scotland,   derives from the Celtic name *Cleschu*, meaning "dear green spot."

Granada, Spain,   was once the name of a Moor kingdom in southern Spain. The name in the Spanish language means "pomegranate," referring to the plants which are plentiful in area.

Grand-Pré, Nova Scotia, Canada,   founded by the French in 1675, is an historic village about fifteen miles northwest of Windsor. It was named for Grandpré, France. *Grand pré* means "large meadow."

The Hague, Netherlands.   Derived from the Dutch term *den Haag*, meaning "the Count," this name goes back to the time when the area was ruled by the counts of the province of Holland.

Halifax, Nova Scotia, Canada,   was founded in 1749 and named for George Montagu-Dunk, second earl of Halifax, who was president of the Board of Trade and a promoter of the town. *Halifax* is an Old English term which means a tress of "holy hair," referring to the tress of a legendary virgin who was murdered, the tress being found hanging upon a tree.

Hamburg, Germany.   Legend tells us that in the year 810, Charlemagne rode with his soldiers up through the forests of Germany to the mouth of the Elbe River. When he reached a place where the river widened into a beautiful harbor, he stopped and built a fortress. The original Anglo-Saxon name of the settlement was *Hammaburg*, "forest city." The hamburger, so popular in the United States, is a variant of Hamburg steak, which was named for this city.

Hamilton, Ontario, Canada, was founded in 1778 by Robert Land, a loyalist from Pennsylvania, who built his cabin where the city now stands. The city took its name from George Hamilton (1787–1835), who settled there in 1813 and attracted other farmers to settle near him.

Hankow, China, means "mouth of the Han River," referring to its location. Alternate spellings are Hangchow and Hangzhou.

Hiroshima, Japan, means "broad island."

Istanbul, Turkey. In about 660 B.C.E., a group of Greeks landed on the northern shore of the Bosporus Sea. They named their new settlement Byzantium, after their leader, Byzas. Byzantium remained a small trading post for almost a thousand years. In 325 C.E., the emperor Constantine built a new Roman capital on the site of ancient Byzantium. This new capital came to be called *Constantinople*, which means "Constantine's city." After the founding of the Turkish Republic in 1930, the city's name was officially changed to Istanbul, a contraction of Constantinople.

Jakarta, Indonesia, was previously called Batavia and was the headquarters of the Dutch East India Company. Now the capital and chief port of Indonesia, and the main railroad center of Java, the name *Jakarta* means "important city."

Jerusalem, Israel, is a Hebrew name meaning "city of peace." Stone tablets recently discovered in Egypt carry the known history of Jerusalem back to 1400 B.C.E. These tablets refer to the city as *Ursalimmu,* an early version of "city of peace." King David captured the city in 1000 B.C.E.

Johannesburg, South Africa, is the largest city of South Africa. Originally a mining town, it was named for Johannes Meyer, a Boer (Dutch) government official. The town was founded after the discovery of gold in the Transvaal province of South Africa.

Khartoum, Sudan, is located between the White Nile and the Blue Nile, on a narrow strip of land shaped somewhat like the tusk of an elephant. The name means "promontory," or, metaphorically, "elephant tusk."

Kingston, Ontario, Canada, founded in 1783, was named in honor of King George III of England by loyalists fleeing the United States.

Kowloon, China, is a suburb of the city of Hong Kong, located on the rocky Kowloon Peninsula. *Kowloon* means "nine dragons." Legend has it that the boy emperor Ti Ping, last ruler of the Sung dynasty (960–1279), named the peninsula when he and his court had to flee from Mongol invaders. A seer had told the boy that he should make his home when he came to a place where nine dragons met. Here, near the South China Sea, a range of hills silhouetted against the sky looked like a row of dragons, and the boy eagerly counted them. To his dismay, there were only eight, but a member of his court told him that since the dragon is the symbol of the emperor, then he must be the ninth dragon. This satisfied the boy and he remained at Kowloon. However, it was not long before the Mongols caught up with them. Then the prime minister, not wanting the boy to be brutally killed, took him on his back and jumped into the sea, thus ending the Sung dynasty.

Kyoto, Japan, means "capital." Kyoto was the capital of Japan before Tokyo.

La Paz, Bolivia. Spanish colonists founded this city in 1548. They named it *La Ciudad de Nuestra Señora de Ayacucho*, which means "the city of Our Lady of Ayacucho." In 1827, Bolivians renamed the city *La Paz de Ayacucho*, which means "the peace of Ayacucho," in commemoration of the 1824 Battle of Ayacucho, which ended Spanish control of Bolivia and Peru.

Libreville, Gabon, was founded by the French in 1849. The name means "free town," and refers to the overthrow of Louis Philippe, king of the French (1773–1850), and the creation of the French republic one year before.

Lima, Peru, was founded by Francisco Pizarro (c. 1474–1541) in 1535 on the site of an ancient temple to the Inca god Rimac. He named it *Ciudad de los Reyes*, "city of the kings," but the Peruvians continued to call the city Rimac. In time, the name Rimac was corrupted to Lima.

Livingstone, Zambia. Now called Maramba, this town was named for Scottish missionary David Livingstone (1813–1873), who spent a great deal of his life exploring Africa and fighting against the slave trade. Maramba, on the Zambezi River, is near Victoria Falls, which were named by Livingstone.

London, England, derives its name from the ancient Anglo-Saxon name Londinion, whose meaning is unknown. Roman invaders built a bridge across the Thames River in the year 43, and called their settlement near the bridge Londinium, based upon the Anglo-Saxon name. Over time, the name was truncated to London.

London, Ontario, Canada, was named for London, England. The river which flows through the city was named the Thames, and the daily paper is called the *Times*, both names also borrowed from the original London.

Louisbourg, Nova Scotia, Canada, lies on the east coast of Cape Breton Island. The French founded this town and named it for King Louis XIV of France (1638–1715).

Madrid, Spain, derives its name from the early Latin name *materita*, meaning "small woods."

Manchuria, China (historical province), was named for the Manchus, the original people who lived there.

Manchuria, encompassing about three provinces, is a name not used in present-day China.

Manitoba, Canada (province), was named for Manitou, the chief god of the Native American tribes who lived in the region.

Marrakech, Morocco. The Arab name means "the adorned."

Memphis, Egypt, was named for Menes, the first Pharaoh to unite the two kingdoms of Egypt in about the year 3000 B.C.E. The Greek version of the name Menes is Memphis.

Mexico City, Mexico. The city was founded on the site of an ancient Aztec city and named for Mexico. The earlier Aztec city was founded by several Aztec tribes who left their home in search of a better one. Legend has it that their chief god told them to look until they found a cactus growing out of a stone, and on this site they would built an ideal city. After searching for a long, long time, these tribes reached a beautiful valley. Standing on the shore of a lake in this valley, they saw an island. On the island they saw a large rock with a cactus growing out of it. An eagle was standing on the cactus, holding a live serpent in its beak. They knew at once that this was the sign for which they had been looking. They built their city on this island and named it *Tenochtitlan*, meaning "place where a cactus grows from a stone." Today, the national flag of Mexico depicts an eagle standing on a cactus holding a snake in its beak, commemorating this ancient legend.

Montevideo, Uruguay, founded in 1726, is the capital and largest city in Uruguay. The name is believed to have come from an exclamation by Magellan as he was sailing by a small coastal hill. Legend has it that he cried, *Monte vide eu*, "I see a hill," and this was elided into its present form.

Montmorency, Quebec, Canada, was named for the duke of Montmorency, who was viceroy of New France from 1619 to 1624.

Montréal, Quebec, Canada, lies on the triangular island of Montréal, at the junction of the Ottawa and St. Lawrence rivers. The backbone of the island is a 769-foot hill, now called Mount Royal. The city was founded by the French in 1642 and named *Ville-Marie de Montréal*, "Mary's town of the royal mountain," later shortened to Montréal. It is the only North American city built around a mountain.

Moose Jaw, Saskatchewan, Canada, is believed to have gotten its name from the fact that the river flowing through the city is shaped like a moose's jaw.

Mostar, Bosnia-Herzegovina. This Slavic name means "bridge-old," and refers to an ancient Roman bridge on the River Narenta.

Munich, Germany, locally called München, derives its name from the old German word meaning "monks," referring to a monastery which was on the site as early as the eighth century.

Nairobi, Kenya. This Swahili name means "sweet water."

Naples, Italy, was founded in 600 B.C.E. on the site of an older Greek settlement called *Parthenope* ("maiden's face"). The new town was named *Neapolis*, meaning "new town." The later Italian name for the city was Napoli, and the English name became Naples, both from shortening.

Nazareth, Israel. This ancient Hebrew name is believed to mean "the guardian."

New Brunswick, Canada (province), was named for King George III of England (1738–1820), who was duke of Brunswick.

New Westminster, British Columbia, Canada, was the first Canadian city on the Pacific coast. Simon Fraser (1776–1862), a British fur trader and explorer, founded the city in 1808. The Royal Engineers named it Queensboro in 1858, but Queen Victoria changed the name to New Westminster a year later, after Westminster, a borough of London, England.

Newcastle-upon-Tyne, England. A new castle was built here in 1080 by Robert, duke of Normandy (1051–1134), to replace the one destroyed by his father, William the Conqueror.

Nova Scotia, Canada (province), is a Latin name meaning "new Scotland." The countryside is similar to Scotland, and the province was settled by many Scottish loyalists.

Ottawa, Ontario, Canada, takes its name from the Ottawa, whose name derives from the Algonquin word *adawe*, meaning "traders." The city was first named Bytown by Colonel John By (1779–1836) of the Royal

Engineers, who used the site as his headquarters while building the Rideau Canal. Queen Victoria declared in 1858 that it should be the new capital of Canada.

Oxford, England, lies on the Thames River about fifty miles northwest of London. The Anglo-Saxon name means "ford of oxen," because there used to be an oxen ford on the site.

Paris, France, was named after a Celtic tribe known as Parisii by the Romans. This early tribe lived on an island in the Seine River. The island is now called *Ile de la Cité* ("island of the city"), because it lies at the heart of Paris.

Prague, Czech Republic. The Czech word *praha*, meaning "threshold," was applied to a reef of rocks in the nearby Moldau River. *Prag* is a German form of *Praha*.

Pretoria, South Africa, was named after Andreis Pretorius, a prominent Afrikaaner leader. Founded in 1855, Pretoria is the capital of the Transvaal province.

Prince Edward Island, Canada, the nation's smallest province, was named for Edward, duke of Kent (1767–1820), son of King George III and future father of Queen Victoria.

Québec, Canada (province), is the French form of an Algonquin word meaning "where the river narrows," because the St. Lawrence River narrows at the site.

Quetzaltenango, Guatemala, derives its name from the quetzal, the national bird of Guatemala. The Atzec name means "place of the quetzal." The second largest city in Guatemala, Quetzaltenango is an important trade center.

Quezon City, Philippines, was named for Manuel Luis Quezon (1878–1944), the first president of the Commonwealth of the Philippines. Quezon City was built next to the city of Manila and served briefly as the nation's capital in 1948.

Quito, Ecuador. This capital city derives its name from *quita*, an indigenous word meaning "deep ravine."

Rangoon, Myanmar. The capital of Myanmar derives its name from a Chinese phrase meaning "war-end." In 1753, a war destroyed the city, but it was rebuilt and given its present name. Another spelling of Rangoon is Yangon.

Río de Janeiro, Brazil, is the second largest city in Brazil. On New Year's Day, 1502, Portuguese navigator André Gonçalves sailed into the bay, which he named *Río de Janeiro*, "river of January." He gave it this name not just because it was January, but because he mistakenly thought the bay was the outlet for a great river. The city was founded in 1565 and named for the bay. Río, as it is often called, has been the capital of Brazil since 1763.

Rome, Italy. Legend tells us that Rome was founded in 753 B.C.E. by twin brothers named Romulus and Remus. After they had been abandoned as infants, they were nursed by a mother wolf. As young men, they decided to build a great city. Romulus wished the Palatine Hill to be the center of the new city, but Remus wanted the nearby Aventine Hill. They agreed to leave the decision to the gods. Each of the young men sat for a whole night on his chosen hill. At daybreak, Remus saw six birds flying over him, but Romulus saw twelve birds at the same time. It was decided that the gods favored Romulus, and he set about building a city on the Palatine Hill. Romulus declared that the new city would be called Rome, after himself. While the city walls were being built, Remus made fun of Romulus by jumping over them, and in anger, Romulus killed him. It is said that Rome is the City of Seven Hills. There are more than seven hills in Rome, and different writers name different hills among the seven, but the Palatine and Aventine hills are always included.

Saint John, New Brunswick, Canada, was named for the St. John River, which was named on the feast day of Saint John the Baptist by Samuel de Champlain in 1604.

Saint John's, Newfoundland, Canada, was named for Saint John the Baptist. Explorer John Cabot (Giovanni Cabato, c. 1450–1499) is said to have discovered the site on the saint's feast day in 1604.

Saint Petersburg, Russia, was founded as the capital of Russia in 1703 by Tsar Peter the Great (1672–1725), who gave the city a fashionable German name in honor of his patron saint. Peter believed that he could make his new capital city as great as the mighty cities of Europe. In 1914, during World War I, the German name was replaced by the equivalent Slavic name Petrograd, to show support for the war cause. In 1924, after the

death of Soviet leader Lenin, the city was renamed
Leningrad by the Soviet government. In 1992, after
the fall of communism, the original name St. Petersburg was restored. Before St. Petersburg was built,
Moscow was the capital of Russia; Moscow again became the capital in 1918.

Salonika, Greece, a shortened form of Thessalonica,
was named for a Macedonian queen who was the half
sister of Alexander the Great. It was founded by Cas-
sander, king of Macedon, about 315 B.C.E., who named
the city for Thessalonica, his wife.

Saragossa, Spain, is a trading center in northeastern
Spain. The city's name comes from *Caesar Augusta*
(Latin, "great emperor"), which over time was elided
to Zaragoza. The English version became Saragossa.
The emperor Augustus gave this, his own name, to the
settlement in 25 B.C.E. when he made it a Roman
colony.

Saskatchewan, Canada (province), was named for the
Saskatchewan River, whose Cree name *kishiska-djiwan*
means "swift current."

Saskatoon, Saskatchewan, Canada, settled in 1882,
took its name from the Native American name for edible red berries that grew along the banks of the Saskatchewan River.

Shanghai, China, is the largest city in China and one
of the largest cities in the world. Its metropolitan population is 12.6 million. Shanghai lies on the banks of
the Huangpu River, at the confluence of the Yangtze

River. The name means "above the sea" and describes the city's location.

Siwa, Egypt. In early times, there was a place called the Siwa Oasis in the Libyan Desert in western Egypt. *Siwa* means "palm-land." The Egyptians gave it this name because there were thousands of palm trees there. The city of Siwa stands today where this ancient oasis was located.

Sofia, Bulgaria, got its name from a medieval church dedicated to Saint Sophia, a Greek name meaning "wisdom."

Stockholm, Sweden, lies upon about twenty islands on the east coast. It was once a city of log buildings made from the great forests around it. Stockholm means "island of the stockade" or "island of logs." After six destructions by fire, however, the people built their capital of granite.

Strasbourg, France, was founded by the Franks in approximately 700 C.E., who named the town *Strateburgum*, meaning "city of roads." Several roads converge at the town. Later, German invaders renamed the city *Strassburg* (German, "city of roads"). When then the French recaptured it, the name became Strasbourg.

Sydney, Australia, was founded as a penal colony in 1788 and named for Thomas Townshend, viscount of Sydney, who at the time was the British home secretary.

Sydney, Nova Scotia, Canada, founded in 1785, was named for Thomas Townshend, viscount of Sydney, British home secretary.

Tblisi, Georgia was founded in 379 C.E. by the Persians, who named the city *Tphilis*, which means "hot springs." The Georgian form of the name is Tblisi. Like many cities, Tblisi was founded on the site of hot mineral springs.

Tegucigalpa, Honduras, is an Aztec name which means "silver hill." Now the capital of Honduras, Tegucigalpa has been the site of extensive gold and silver mining since the sixteenth century.

Tientsin, China. The name means "celestial palace."

Tokyo, Japan, was founded in 1456 and named Yeddo. The name was changed in 1868 to *Tokyo*, which means "eastern capital." Prior to this time, Kyoto was the sole capital of Japan.

Tombouctou, Mali, formerly Timbuktu, is said to derive its name from a legendary woman named Buktu. The name means "place of Buktu."

Toronto, Ontario, Canada, derives its name from the Wyandot word *thorontohen*, meaning "place of meeting." The term is thought to indicate the crossing of two major trails in the area, and a common conference site of many local tribes. This name was given to the harbor as early as 1615. In 1793, the name York was given to this growing city, and the name was changed to Toronto in 1834.

Valetta, Malta. Valetta is the capital and chief seaport of Malta. It was founded in 1565 and named for Jean de la Valette, grand master of the Knights of Malta.

Valparaiso, Chile, is the nation's principal seaport. The Spanish name derives from *valle,* "valley," and *paraíso,* "paradise."

Vancouver, British Columbia, Canada, was named for the English sea captain George Vancouver (1757–1798), who explored the area in 1792.

Veracruz, Mexico, was founded in 1519 by the Spanish as a port. The city was named *La Villa Rica de la Vera Cruz,* meaning "the rich city of the true cross." As is the case with many Spanish city names, it was later shortened.

Windsor, Ontario, Canada, was named for Windsor, England, or the royal Windsor Castle. The name Windsor derives from old English, and means either "winding shore" or "willow-basket tree."

Winnipeg, Manitoba, Canada, derives its name from the Cree words *win nipi,* meaning "muddy water." The river flowing through the city and emptying into Lake Winnipeg is called the Red River, and its waters have a muddy, red appearance. The city of Winnipeg is not actually near the river or the lake which share its name.

Yukon Territory, Canada, was named for the Yukon River, which derived its name from the Native American term *yukon-na,* meaning "big river."

5

Continents

Africa

The Phoenicians, who lived in the area of present-day Lebanon some three thousand years ago, were great adventurers. Sailing away from their native land, they visited the entire coast of northern Africa, from Egypt to as far west as Gibraltar. Their voyages west of Egypt brought them into contact with many other peoples.

The people they found on the northern coast of what is now Africa called themselves the Ifri. The Phoenicians traded with the Ifri and set up colonies in Tunisia that later became cities. The Phoenicians named that part of the Mediterranean coast *Ifrikiya*, which meant "land of the Ifri." Later the Romans called the coast Afrika.

At first, this name applied only to the area where the Ifri lived, but as time passed, it came to apply to more of the coast, then to some of the interior, and finally the name Africa was applied to the entire continent.

When the Phoenicians first came to what is now Libya, Tunisia, and Morocco, they referred to the land as the Dark Continent, not because the people who lived there were dark, but because they were ignorant of what most of its interior was like.

190

North and South America

These two continents were named for Italian explorer Amerigo Vespucci (1451–1512), who explored the coasts of Brazil, Uruguay, and Peru between 1499 and 1502. They were not named for Christopher Columbus because he never realized that he had discovered continents which were unknown to the Europeans. Columbus died thinking he had found India, which is why he called the indigenous people Indians.

Amerigo Vespucci was a scholarly young man in the court of Lorenzo de Medici of Florence, Italy. He realized that Columbus had discovered a new continent, which he named *Mundus Novus* (Latin, "new world"). Vespucci became a sailor and made four voyages to the New World, but only two can be substantiated. He journeyed not as a leader but as a sailor, and being an educated man, he wrote of his experiences.

In 1507, a German mapmaker, Martin Waldseemüller, made a map of the New World. Waldseemüller wanted a name for the new lands that had been discovered. He had heard of the voyages of Americus Vespusius, as he was called in Latin, and decided to give his name to the New World. He wrote the name America on the map. Many of these maps were sold, which gave publicity to the name.

At first, the name applied only to that part of the southern continent along which Vespucci had sailed. In 1538, mapmaker Gerhardus Mercator designated a North America and a South America on his map of the world, and soon these names were accepted for the new continents.

Antarctica

The name means "opposite the Arctic." The name Arctic comes from the Greek word *arktos*, which means "bear."

The Greeks gave this name to a great northern constellation, which we call Ursa Major, or the Great Bear. The Greek word *arktikos*, meaning "land of the bear," became our name for the cold Far North, the Arctic.

The Antarctic continent is the highest, coldest, windiest, loneliest continent in the world. It is larger than Australia, and much of the continent has never been explored. Its population, on average about three thousand, consists only of researchers from other countries.

The region near the South Pole has a hard, long winter when the sun is never seen. It has a long summer, too—when the sun never sets. Only some areas of Antarctica have sunrise and sunset throughout the year.

The winters in this land of the Far South are the coldest on earth. In 1957, a low of minus 102.1 degrees Fahrenheit was recorded. Even in summer, the temperature seldom goes above freezing. Most of the continent is perpetually covered with a mile-thick layer of ice and snow, and aprons of snow reach out into the ocean. Through the ice, great volcanic mountains rise, the largest one taller than any mountain in the United States. Steam rises from the top of Mount Erebus, the best known of Antarctica's volcanoes.

Asia

The ancient Greeks knew of two major continents, one to the east of the Aegean Sea and one to the west. They called the eastern continent Assu, which comes from the older Semitic word *assu*, meaning "east." The name Assu became the name Asia.

Australia

The name Australia derives from the Latin name *Terra Australis*, meaning "southern land." For centuries before

European explorers actually located Australia, they theorized that there was a major land mass in the southern Pacific Ocean. They called this unknown place *Terra Australis Incognito*, or "land-southern-unknown." When the continent was finally identified, it was named *Australia*, "southland."

Australia is also called the Land Down Under, because it is south of equator. It is winter there when we have summer in the United States, and night when we have day. Except for Antarctica, Australia is the last continent to be settled by Europeans.

Europe

The continent of Europe was named by the ancient Greeks, who named it for its position west of the Aegean Sea. They called it Ereb, from the Semitic word *ereb*, meaning "west."

Later the people in Greece and the surrounding area learned that Europe was not really a continent, because it was connected to Asia north of the Aegean Sea. Europe is actually a peninsula on the continent of Asia. However, since the original Greek vantage point made Europe appear to be a separate continent, we continue to call it one.

6

Oceans and Seas

Adriatic Sea. The Adriatic Sea was named for Adria, once a flourishing Roman seaport.

Aegean Sea. The Aegean is an arm of the Mediterranean, located between Greece and Asia Minor. It is four hundred miles long and two hundred miles wide. The sea was named for Aegeus, king of Athens. Legend has it that Aegeus's son Theseus was sailing home from a harrowing adventure, and he was to signal to his father with a white sail if he was still alive. If the ship flew a black sail, Aegeus would know that his son had been slain. Unfortunately, Theseus forgot to raise a white sail, and Aegeus, seeing the ship's black sail in the distance, drowned himself in the sea.

Antarctic Ocean. The waters around the continent of Antarctica are called the Antarctic Ocean. The name Antarctic derives from the Greek word *anti*, meaning "opposite," added to Arctic. The winters in this land of the Far South are the coldest on earth.

Arctic Ocean. The Arctic Ocean derives its name from the Greek term *Arktos*, the name of a northern constellation commonly called Ursa Major or the Great Bear.

Atlantic Ocean. The ancient Greeks named the Atlantic Ocean after the Atlas Mountains, in what is now Morocco, at the edge of what was to them the known world.

Baltic Sea. This sea derives its name from the old Norse word *belti*, "belt," a poetic reference to the sea which surrounds the earth. Another possibility is the Lithuanian *baltas*, "white," referring to the chalk cliffs of the islands in the sea.

Barents Sea. This sea lies to the north of Europe, in an area between Norway and Russia. The sea was named for Willem Barents (c. 1550–1597), a Dutch navigator who explored it from 1594 to 1596.

Bering Sea. Located between Alaska and Siberia, the Bering Sea was named for Iran Ivanovich Bering (1681–1741), also known as Vitus Bering, a Danish explorer employed by Russia.

Black Sea. The Black Sea is a body of water between Europe and the Middle East. It is called the Black Sea because heavy fogs make the water look dark during the winter. The Russian name for it is *Chernoye More*, also meaning "black sea."

Caribbean Sea. The Caribbean Sea lies south of the Gulf of Mexico and southwest of the West Indies. When Columbus sailed through the region, Native Americans attacked his party with poisoned arrows, killing one of his men. Columbus then called them *Caribales*, meaning "savages." European invaders later exterminated the Native Americans and replaced them with slaves taken from Africa. The Caribbean Sea derives its name from the term *Caribales*, shortened to *Carib*.

Coral Sea. This sea is part of the Pacific Ocean between the northeast coast of Australia, the Solomon Islands, and Vanuatu. The reefs along the western shores of the Coral Sea have the finest specimens of coral to be found in the world.

Dead Sea. The Dead Sea is well named because it is so salty that nothing can live in its waters. Around the sea are barren shores. Gases that bubble up through the water give the area an unpleasant odor.

Indian Ocean. This ocean took its name from India, which in turn took its name from the Indus River.

Ionian Sea. The Ionian Sea is a part of the Mediterranean Sea that was named for the Greek nymph Io. According to ancient legend, Jupiter changed Io into a heifer so that his wife, Juno, would not guess that he was making love to a beautiful nymph. But Juno found out and sent a gadfly to torment Io, who tried to escape by swimming the sea that came to be named for her.

Mediterranean Sea. The Romans named this sea. Its name comes from the Latin words *medius*, "middle," and *terra*, "earth," possibly meaning "between the land." This long sea, nearly enclosed by land, was the middle of the world that the Greeks and Romans knew.

It served as a highway for their ships to travel to surrounding countries.

Pacific Ocean. The Pacific was named in 1520 by Portuguese navigator Ferdinand Magellan (1480–1521) for its calmness, after an unusually peaceful voyage upon its waters. The Spanish word *pacífico* means "peaceful." It just happened to be peaceful while he was sailing. Actually, it is the most turbulent of all the oceans.

Sargasso Sea. The Sargasso Sea derives its name from *sargoco*, one of the Portuguese words for "seaweed." The word originally meant "grape," because the small bunches of seaweed resembled grapes, but it came to mean "seaweed." So much seaweed floated in this area of the Atlantic that it was a hazard to ships.

Sea of Galilee. The Sea of Galilee got its name from the province known as Galilee, which derives its name from the ancient Hebrew term *Galil haggoyim*, meaning "land of foreigners," referring to the land north of Israel. Galilee was also called Gennesarat, for the plain that lies to the northwest, and sometimes Tiberius, for a city on its shore named for Tiberius Caesar.

Tasman Sea. This sea was named for Abel Janszoon Tasman, a Dutch navigator. The island Tasmania was also named for him.

Yellow Sea. The waters along the banks here are a yellow, muddy color, and the Chinese have named this part of the ocean *Huang Hai*, meaning "yellow sea."

7

Bays and Lakes

Agassiz Lake is on the border between North Dakota and Minnesota. It was formed by the melting of the continental ice sheet some ten thousand years ago. It is 250 miles wide and 700 miles long. The lake was named in 1879 in honor of Louis Agassiz (1807–1873), a Swiss-American scientist who studied glaciers and discovered the ice ages.

Albano, Lake. This lake lies in the crater of an extinct volcano in Italy just outside Rome. It is more than five hundred feet deep. The ancient Romans spent vacations at this lake, known then as *Albanus Lacus* (Latin, "white lake").

Albert, Lake. One of the sources of the Nile River, this lake was discovered in 1864 by Sir Samuel Baker (1821–1893) and named for Albert, prince of Saxe-Coburg (1819–1861), husband of Queen Victoria. Located on the border between Uganda and Zaïre, it is now called Lake Mobutu Sese Soko.

Baffin Bay. In 1616, William Baffin (1584–1622), an English navigator, sailed far north along the northeastern coast of North America and became the first European to visit this bay that now bears his name. Baffin Bay on the coast of Texas was named for the first Baffin Bay.

Bay of Biscay. The Bay of Biscay lies on the western coast of France and the northern coast of Spain. It gets its name from the Basques, a people who live along its rocky Spanish shore.

Champlain, Lake. Lying between New York and Vermont and touching Québec, this lake was named for Samuel de Champlain (1567–1635), the French explorer who founded Québec and who was the first European (1609) to reach the lake.

Charles, Lake. Located in Louisiana, this lake was named for Spaniard Carlos Salia, who settled in the area in 1780 and then promoted the exploitation of the many pine trees. Salia later adopted the French form of his name, Charles.

Chesapeake Bay lies on the Maryland coast, extending into Virginia. Its name derives from the Algonquin village named *Chesepiooc*, believed to mean "on the big bay."

Cumberland, Lake. An artificial lake in south central Kentucky, Lake Cumberland is located on the Cumberland River, from which it derives its name.

Edward, Lake. Welsh explorer Henry Stanley (1841–1904) named this lake in 1889 for Edward, Prince of Wales, who later became King Edward VII of England (1841–1910). Located on the border between Zaïre and Uganda, Lake Edward covers 820 square miles and is one of the sources of the Nile River.

Erie, Lake.   One of the Great Lakes, it was named after a local tribe whom the Iroquois called the *Erieehronos*. The name means "people of the panther," sometimes translated as "cat nation." The French settlers borrowed this name and called it *Lac du Chat*, "lake of the cat." Later, British settlers began calling it Lake Erie.

Finger Lakes.   This New York chain of inland lakes, including Seneca and Cayuga, were so named because they resemble the fingers of an open hand. There are about eleven of them.

George, Lake.   Located in eastern New York, this lake was named by General William Johnston in 1755 for King George III of England (1738–1820).

Great Bear Lake.   One of the largest lakes in North America, Great Bear Lake covers twelve thousand square miles in the Northwest Territories of Canada. It received its name because of its large size and because there are many bears that live along its shores.

Great Slave Lake.   Located in Canada's Northwest Territories, this lake was named for a tribe who lived in the area, called Slave by their enemies, the Cree. In 1771, English explorer Samuel Hearne (1745–1792) became the first European to reach the lake.

Hudson Bay,   a vast inland bay in northeast Canada, was named for Henry Hudson (?–1611), an English navigator and the first European to enter the bay and explore the river that both bear his name.

Huron, Lake. One of the Great Lakes, it was named for the Wyandot, a Native American tribe whom the French unflatteringly labeled *Huron*, meaning "rough ones."

Itasca Lake. The source of the Mississippi River, this Minnesota lake was named by Henry Rowe Schoolcraft (1793–1864), who discovered it in 1862. He coined the name from the Latin words *veritas*, "truth," and *caput*, "head," taking the last letters of *veritas* and the first letters of *caput*, thus making a name meaning "true head" or "true source." However, a Native American legend tells that Hiawatha had a beautiful daughter named Iteska, who was kidnapped by the rulers of the underworld, and that her tears started the Mississippi River. Some believe the lake was named for her.

James Bay is the southern arm of Hudson Bay. The bay was named for Thomas James, an English navigator who explored the bay in 1631 and again in 1633 while trying to discover the Northwest Passage.

Junaluska, Lake. This North Carolina lake was named for Junaluska (c. 1755–1858), a Cherokee chief who fought with General Andrew Jackson in the Creek wars (1813–1814). His name, which means "he tries repeatedly but fails," was given to him when he bragged he would wipe out the Creeks in battle but failed to do so.

Lake of the Ozarks. This lake was formed in 1931 by the Bagnell Dam on the Osage River. It winds for 130 miles within the Ozark Mountains for which it is named. *Ozark* is derived from the French descriptive *aux arcs*, pronounced "oh's arks," meaning "in the land of the Arkansas." This lake has a thirteen-hundred-mile shoreline dotted with more than three hundred resorts.

Lake of the Woods. Lying on the boundary between Minnesota and Ontario, and also touching Manitoba, this lake covers 1,485 square miles, most of which are in Ontario. It was named for the forests that cover its hilly shores and islands.

Maggiore, Lake. This lake is located in Italy, where *maggiore* means "greater."

Memphremagog, Lake. Located on the border between Vermont and Québec, this lake derives its name from an Algonquin name meaning "wide expanse of water."

Michigan, Lake. One of the Great Lakes, it derives its name from the Fox term *mesikami*, meaning "large lake," or from the Ojibway name *michi-gama*, meaning "great water." Both names are Algonquin.

Monterey, Bay. This California bay was named in honor of Gaspar de Acevedey Zuñiga, conde de Monterey (1560–1606), viceroy of New Spain.

Morey, Lake. Located in Vermont, this lake was named for Samuel Morey, who invented the first steamboat years before Robert Fulton. Fulton gave Morey $100,000 worth of worthless stock for the invention. In 1826, Morey patented an internal combustion engine, the forerunner of the gasoline engine.

Narragansett Bay is a narrow arm of the Atlantic that extends twenty-eight miles into the state of Rhode Island. Its name derives from *Nanhiggonsick,* an Algonquin tribal name meaning "back and forth," or possibly "people of the point."

Nasser, Lake. Located in Egypt, this lake was named for Egyptian president Gamal Abdel Nasser (1918–1970).

None Such. Located in Massachusetts, this small lake was given this flattering name, which means "none better."

Okeechobee, Lake. This Florida lake derives its name from the Hitchiti words *oki,* "water," and *chobi,* "big." The largest lake in the southern United States, the lake is located in the Everglades, about thirty-five miles west of the Atlantic coast.

Oneida, Lake. Located in New York, this lake was named for the Oneida, one of the Five Nations of the Iroquois, whose name means "stone people," referring to their bravery. The Oneida once had a village on its shores.

Ontario, Lake. The smallest and most eastern of the Great Lakes, the name of Lake Ontario comes from the Iroquois words *ontare,* "lake," and *io,* "beautiful."

Placid, Lake. Located in the Adirondack Mountains of New York, Lake Placid was named for its peaceful waters.

Ponchartrain, Lake. Located in Louisiana, just north of New Orleans, Lake Ponchartrain was named for Louis, comte de Ponchartrain (1643–1727), a member of King Louis XIV's cabinet who was admired by the French settlers of the region.

Powell, Lake. One of the largest artificially created lakes in the world, Lake Powell lies in the basin of Glen Canyon on the border between Arizona and Utah. The lake was named for American geologist John Wesley Powell (1834–1902), who explored and named the canyon in 1870.

Pyramid Lake, in Nevada, was named in 1844 by explorer John Frémont (1813–1890) for the giant rock formation in the lake which, he said, "resembled the Great Pyramid of Cheops."

Quake Lake. This lake came into being in August of 1959 when a big earthquake hit Yellowstone National Park in Montana. A whole mountain collapsed into the Madison River, and this new lake was born.

Reelfoot Lake. On December 16, 1811, a great earthquake occurred in northwest Tennessee, resulting in almost fifteen thousand acres of Cherokee and Chickasaw land being inundated with water from the Mississippi. Andrew Jackson and his soldiers were traveling down the Mississippi at the time to fight in the Battle of New Orleans. Their boats went backward for a few days until the lake was filled. It was an awesome time for the Cherokee and Chickasaw. As the Mississippi swept in, many lives were lost.

Reelfoot Lake got its name from a Chickasaw known as Kalopin, or Reelfoot, because of his irregular gait.

Legend has it that Kalopin's people would not give him a wife because he was clubfooted, so he went to the Choctaws, who did give him a bride. Then, during the wedding celebration, the catastrophe happened, and Kalopin and his new bride, Laughing Eyes, were buried beneath the onrushing waters.

Rudolph, Lake. Located in northeastern Kenya, this lake was named in 1888 by Austrian explorer Count Pal Teleki in honor of Rudolph, crown prince of Austria (1858–1889).

Salton Sea. The Salton Sea, actually a lake in California, lies in the Salton Sink, a low-lying area in the desert that was once covered with salt. In 1905 to 1907, the diversion controls of the Colorado River broke and flooded the depression, creating a 450-square-mile salt lake. The descriptive name was coined from the word *salt.*

San Julian Bay. Magellan explored this sheltered bay on the coast of Argentina on Saint Julian's day in 1520. Native people there looked so large to him that he named them Patagonians, which means "big feet." The name Patagonia is now applied to a region of Argentina near the southern tip of South America.

Sturgeon Bay, an arm of Green Bay, Wisconsin, took its name from the plentiful sturgeon fishing that the bay made possible in early days. So many sturgeon were once caught there that they were piled on the shore like cordwood.

Superior, Lake. One of the Great Lakes, it was named *Lac Superieur* by French explorers in the seventeenth century. The name means "upper lake" and refers to its position north of Lake Huron. The lake covers 31,800 square miles, an area greater than that of South Carolina. Its greatest length from east to west is 350 miles, and its greatest width is 180 miles. At its deepest point, the lake is 1,333 feet deep. Since it is the largest and deepest body of fresh water in the world, many English-speaking people take its name to mean "greatest."

Tahoe, Lake. On the border between California and Nevada, this lake was named in 1862 with the Washo (Native American) name meaning "big water."

Victoria, Lake. The largest lake in Africa and the second largest freshwater lake in the world, it was named in 1858 by English explorer John Hanning Speke (1827–1864) in honor of Queen Victoria. Lake Victoria lies on the border between Tanganyika, Uganda, and Kenya, and covers an area of 26,800 square miles.

Walker Lake. This Nevada lake was named for James R. Walker, an early frontier guide who is credited with its discovery.

Wentworth, Lake. Located in New Hampshire, Lake Wentworth was named for Governor Benning Wentworth, who built here the first true "summer home" ever erected in the United States.

Winnebago, Lake. The largest lake in Wisconsin, Winnebago derives its name from the Winnebago, a Dakota tribe whose name is believed to mean "fish eaters."

Winnipesaukee Lake   is the largest lake in New Hampshire. A legend explains how it got its name. Kona, a Native American warrior, loved Ellacaye, daughter of Chief Ahanton. Although Kona and Ahanton were enemies, Kona went to Ahanton to ask to marry his daughter. This bravery was admired so much by the chief that he permitted the marriage. Watching the happy couple paddle across a nearby lake, Ahanton felt the omen must be good, and he said, "That all the tribes may know of peace between us, may these waters be called Winnipesaukee, the smile of the Great Spirit." This is only one of the many legends that tell how the lake was given its name; over one hundred spellings and dozens of possible translations of the name have been put forth.

8

Rivers

Amazon River. Among the Greek legends, there are stories of strong, brave women warriors called Amazons. Spanish explorer Vicente Pinzón sailed into the Amazon River's hundred-mile-wide mouth in 1500, and it is believed that he named the river after the legendary Amazon warriors, because he saw what he thought were Amazons along the banks. The Amazon River is the highest-volume river in the world. It flows from Peru through Brazil and empties into the Atlantic Ocean.

Cache la Poudre River. This river in Colorado is said to have taken its name from a group of French trappers who had to lighten their wagons in a snowstorm, and hid their supplies near the river. Included in the supplies was a very large store of powder, leading to the name *Cache la Poudre* ("hiding place of powder"), and the river has been called Cache la Poudre ever since.

Chattahoochee River. This river rises in the Blue Ridge Mountains in Georgia and flows along the borders of Alabama and Florida. Its name comes from the

Creek term *chattahoochee,* meaning "marked rocks," referring to painted stones found in river.

Chickasawhay River. This river in Mississippi derives its name from the Choctaw name *Tchikahaé,* recorded by the French in 1732. The original meaning is unknown, but over time the name was stretched to resemble the tribal name Chickasaw.

Christina River. Located in Delaware, this river was named by Swedish colonists, who in 1638 built Fort Christina along the river, which was named in honor of Queen Christina of Sweden (1626–1689).

Churchill River, in Newfoundland, was named in 1965 for British statesman Sir Winston Churchill (1874–1965). Before that time, it was called the Hamilton River.

Coal River, in West Virginia, was named in 1742 for the abundance of coal in the area.

Columbia River. This river flows south from British Columbia to form the border between Washington and Oregon. It was named in 1792 by explorer Captain Robert Gray (1755–1806) after his ship *Columbia.*

Cooper River. This South Carolina river was named for Anthony Ashley Cooper, earl of Shaftesbury, a proprietor. The Ashley River was also named for him.

Cumberland River. Flowing through Kentucky and Tennessee, this river was named for the county of Cumberland, England. The name was also popularized by English military leader Prince William Augustus, duke of Cumberland (1721–1765), who was admired for defeating an army of Scottish rebels in Britain in 1745.

Cuyahoga River. This river, which flows through Cleveland, Ohio, derives its name from the Iroquois word *cuyahaga*, meaning "crooked."

Danube River. This river flows through from Germany across Europe to the Black Sea. It derives its name from the Celtic word *dan*, "strong," with a formative suffix.

Euphrates River. This river, flowing through Iraq, derives its name from the Greek adaptation of the Semitic name *Hufrat*, meaning "great water."

Fraser River. The 1792 discovery of this British Columbian river is credited to the Canadian fur trader Sir Alexander Mackenzie (c. 1764–1820), who was the first European to cross Canada by land. The river is named for Simon Fraser, a German Canadian trader who followed the river to the sea in 1808. The Fraser River was the scene of a famous gold rush in 1858.

Huang River. The Chinese name of this river is *Hwang Ho*, meaning "yellow river," referring to the large amounts of soft yellow earth carried by its waters. Emptying into the Yellow Sea, this river is so shallow that only small boats can travel on it.

Hudson River. This New York river empties into the Atlantic Ocean through New York City. It was named for Henry Hudson (?–1611), the first English explorer to traverse the river.

Indus River. The most important river of southwestern Asia derives its name from the Sanskrit word *sindhu,* meaning "river." The Indus River gave India its name.

James River. Located in Virginia and flowing through Jamestown, this river was named for King James I of England (1566–1625), who chartered the first English colony in New World.

Jefferson River. When Lewis and Clark made their expedition to the Northwest (1804–1806), they named this Montana river in honor of their patron, President Thomas Jefferson.

Jordan River flows into the Dead Sea, which, at 1286 feet below sea level, is one of the lowest places on the surface of the earth. The name Jordan derives from the Hebrew word meaning "descender."

Judith River. This Montana river was discovered by Lewis and Clark. William Clark named it for Judith Hancock, the sweetheart he left behind in Virginia. A cousin of Lewis, she later became Clark's wife.

Kennebec River. Located in Maine, this river derives its name from the Algonquin term *kini beki,* meaning "long lake" or "long reach."

Mackenzie River. Located in Canada, this is the second longest river in North America. It is 2,635 miles long from its mouth to its most distant source. The river was named for Canadian explorer and trader Sir Alexander Mackenzie (c. 1764–1820).

Madeira River.   This river in Brazil is the largest branch of the Amazon. Its Portuguese name means "wood," referring to the large amount of driftwood floating on its waters.

Merrimack River.   Located in New Hampshire, this river derives its name from the Algonquin name *meramec*, meaning "swift water" or "deep place."

Miami River.   This Ohio river was named for the Miami, a Native American group who lived along its banks. Miami derives from the Ojibway word *oumaumeg*, meaning "people who live on the peninsula." The Miami name in Florida comes from a different source.

Mississippi River.   The longest river in North America derives its name from the Algonquin words *mescha*, "great," and *cebe*, "water."

Mobile River.   Located in Alabama, and emptying into Mobile Bay through the city of Mobile, this river derives its name from the *Moila*, a Native American band whose name is believed to mean "canoe paddlers." The French Canadian explorer Jean-Baptiste le Moyne recorded the name as Mobile.

Mohawk River.   This New York river, the largest branch of the Hudson, was named for an Iroquois tribe whom other Native Americans called *Mohawk*, meaning "cannibals."

Monongahela River. Flowing from West Virginia to Pennsylvania, this tributary of the Ohio River derives it name from the Algonquin *men-aun-ge-hilla*, meaning "river with the sliding banks," referring to the many landslides that occur along its shores.

Montmorency River. This Canadian river was named for Xavier de Laval Montmorency, the first bishop of Québec.

Nile River. The ancient Egyptians called this river *Hapi*, "the river," and personified it in a deity characterized by both masculine and feminine features. In early Egyptian literature, the river was referred to as the Nachal of Egypt, an early Semitic or Phoenician name from which we get the name Nile.

Two major branches of the Nile are called the White Nile and the Blue Nile. The **White Nile**, originating in Lake Victoria, was so named because it carries a great deal of white soil in its waters. The **Blue Nile** originates in Lake Tana, among the mountains of Ethiopia, and its clear, silt-free water reflects the sky, giving it a blue appearance and thus its name.

The Nile is the longest river in the world, flowing for 4,160 miles, nearly the width of the United States. The Nile Delta, in northern Egypt, was named by the Greeks because it resembles the Greek letter delta, which is in the shape of an equilateral triangle. This is the general shape of most river deltas, because of their tendency to branch out at the mouth due to the buildup of sediment.

Nolichucky River. This North Carolina–Tennessee river derives its name from the Cherokee word *none-*

chunkeh, meaning "rushing water" or "place of spruce trees."

Oconaluftee River. This North Carolina river derives its name from the Cherokee term that means "soapy water." Another possibility is that it was named for a Cherokee village, the name meaning "near the river."

Orange River. This river in South Africa was named in the 1600s by Dutch settlers for the House of Orange, the royal family of the Netherlands.

Ottawa River. This Ontario river was named for the Ottawa, a Native American tribe whose name means "traders." The Ottawa lived in the Great Lakes region of what is now the United States and Canada.

Pascagoula River. The Leaf and Chickasawhay rivers unite not many miles from the Gulf of Mexico in Mississippi to form the Pascagoula, known picturesquely as the Singing River. The singing sound that resembles the buzzing of a swarm of bees can be heard on summer evenings. The sound is made by the rushing of water over pebbly stones. *Pascagoula* is a Caddo name meaning "singing river."

The Native Americans have a legend to explain the singing noise. There were once two tribes that went to war over a princess who married into an enemy tribe. When the young chief saw that the battle had turned against him and his bride, they along with their people walked into the river and committed suicide. The legend says that the singing noise is their song of death as it rises forever from the depths of the water.

Penobscot River. Located in Maine, this river derives its name from the Algonquin term *penobskeag,* meaning "rocky river" or "rocky place," referring to a rocky stretch of the river near Bangor.

Potomac River. Flowing south from West Virginia through Washington, D.C., and emptying into Chesapeake Bay, this river got its name from the Iroquois name recorded in 1608 as *Patawomeck*, meaning "where goods are brought in." Iroquois, Powhatan, and Leni-Lenapé did much trading in this area before European settlers drove them out.

Purgatoire River. The original Spanish name for this Colorado river was *Las Animas*, "the souls," referring to a group of Spanish explorers who died near its banks in 1595. Since they had no priest with them to give them the last rites, their souls were believed to have gone to purgatory. Later the name became El Purgatoria. The French later adopted the name and called the river Purgatoire. The local name, Picketwire, is a corruption of Purgatoire.

Red River. This river flows from New Mexico along the border of Texas, emptying into the Mississippi River in Louisiana. It was named for the red clay soil that forms the banks of its upper basin.

Río Grande. This river forms part of the Texas-Mexico border. Its Spanish name means "great river." The Río Grande has been described as "a mile wide and a foot deep—too thin to plow and too thick to drink."

Río Negro. This stream that enters the Amazon is called Río Negro, "black river," due to the black mud carried by its waters.

Río Tinto. This river in southern Spain was named *Río Tinto*, "red river," for the color of the soil upon its banks.

Saint John's River. This New Brunswick river was named for Saint John the Baptist by French explorer Samuel de Champlain (1567–1635), who first encountered it on the feast day of Saint John.

Saint Marys River. This river connects Lake Superior to Lake Huron, on the border between Michigan and Ontario. It was named for Saint Mary, mother of Christ.

Schoolcraft River. This small northern branch of the Mississippi River was named in honor of Henry Rowe Schoolcraft (1793–1864), who discovered Itaska Lake, the true source of the Mississippi. An ethnologist and author, Schoolcraft is credited with coining many names which sound like authentic Native American words, including Itaska.

Seine. This is the main river of Paris, France. Its name derives from the Roman name *Sequana*, meaning unknown.

Shenandoah River. This river flows through Virginia and West Virginia, joining the Potomac River at Harpers Ferry. Its Algonquin name, *shind-han-dowi*, means "spruce stream," although some translate it as "beautiful daughter of the stars."

Singing River. See *Pascagoula River*.

Snake River. This tributary of Columbia River forms the border of Idaho. It was named after a Shoshone tribe called the Snake.

Susquehanna River. This picturesque river flows through New York, Pennsylvania, and Maryland. It was named for the Susquehanna, an Iroquois tribe who lived along its banks in the seventeenth century. New England pioneer Captain John Smith (c. 1580–1631) recorded the name in 1608 as Sasquesahanough. The precise meaning of the name is unknown.

Thames River. Flowing through London, England, the name comes from a Celtic word which has been variously translated as "broad river," "dark," "smooth," or "tranquil." Early Roman invaders borrowed the Celtic name and called it the Tamesis River.

Tigris River. Along with the Euphrates, this river forms a fertile valley in Iraq which has been the site of human settlement for thousands of years. The ancient Medes name *Tigris* means "arrow," denoting the swiftness of its current.

Tombigbee River. This river rises in Mississippi, but the largest part of it flows through Alabama. The name derives from the Choctaw words *itombi*, "coffin," and *ikbi*, "makers," referring to a group of Choctaw who disposed of the dead.

Tweed. The River Tweed divides Scotland and England. The name derives from the Anglo-Saxon *tuedd*, meaning "border." Tweed cloth was first manufactured in southern Scotland.

Wabash River. This river forms the border between Indiana and Illinois and is a tributary of the Ohio River. It derives its name from the Miami phrase *wahba-shik-ki*, meaning "pure white," referring to a limestone bed in the river.

Yangtze River. This Chinese river's name means "long." The largest river in China, its name is also spelled Yangtse Kiang or Chang Jiang, the word *kiang* or *jiang* meaning "river."

Yazoo River. A tributary of the Mississippi, this river gets its name from the Yazoo, a Chickasaw or Choctaw band whose name is believed to mean "death."

Yellowstone River. This river rises near the Continental Divide in northwestern Wyoming, flows through Yellowstone National Park in Montana, and joins the Missouri River. Its original name was *Mitsia-dazi*, a Native American term meaning "yellow rock river." French traders translated the name and called it *Roche Jaune*, "yellow stone." Both names refer to a mighty yellow rock near the mouth of the river.

9

Islands

Alcatraz. This island in San Francisco Bay, a former federal penitentiary, is now a tourist attraction. It was named 1775 for the many pelicans which flourish there. *Alcatraz* is a Spanish word meaning "pelican."

Aleutian Islands. This group of islands off the Alaska coast is named for the Aleut, the tribal name of the Native American inhabitants. The meaning of the name unknown.

Alexander Archipelago. This group of islands lies along the southern extension of the coast of Alaska. They were named in 1867 in honor of Tsar Alexander I of Russia (1777–1825).

Antelope Island is the largest island in the Great Salt Lake in Utah. It was named by explorer John Frémont, who killed several antelope there in 1845.

Antigua. This Caribbean island was named by Columbus in 1493, after Santa Maria la Antigua, a chapel in Seville, Spain. The chapel's name means "old Saint Mary," and *antigua* means "antique" or "old."

Azores.   In the Portuguese language, Azores is spelled *Açores* and means "hawks." The many hawks living on the islands gave them their name.

Balearic Islands.   This archipelago of five Spanish islands in the Mediterranean Sea got its name from the Greek word meaning "to throw." In ancient times, the people of the Balearic Islands were famous for their skill with the sling. They served in the armies of the Carthaginians, the Greeks, and the Romans.

Baranof Island.   This island lies in the Alexander Archipelago of Alaska. It was named in 1805 for Alexander Andreievich Baranof (1746–1819), first governor of Russian America. The Tlingit name for the island, Sitka, was given to its largest settlement.

Belle Isle.   Located in the Detroit River, this picturesque little spot was once known as Hog Island, possibly for a group of wild pigs that were found there. *Belle Isle*, a French name meaning "beautiful island," is a name found in many places throughout North America. However, some believe this island was named for Isabella Cass, daughter of Michigan Governor Lewis Cass (1782–1866).

Bermuda Islands.   These islands in the Atlantic were named for Juan Bermudez, a Spanish merchant who was shipwrecked on them in 1515. Bermudez made his way back to Spain with glowing reports about the islands, but the Spanish were not interested in them because the reefs were so dangerous to ships. In 1609, English navigator Sir George Somers was shipwrecked there, and since that time the Bermudas have belonged to England.

Block Island. This island off the coast of Rhode Island was named in 1614 by Dutch explorer Adriaen Block for himself.

Bougainville, the largest of the Solomon Islands, is part of the territory of New Guinea. French navigator Louis Antonine de Bougainville (1729–1811) discovered the Soloman Islands in 1768.

Calendar Islands. This group of islands is located in Casco Bay, off the coast of Maine. It is said there are 365 isles and islets in the bay, one for each day of the year, which is why they are called the Calendar Islands.

Canary Islands. The Spaniards discovered a breed of large dogs here in 1492 and named the islands *Gran Canaria*, meaning "great dogs." The English name became Canary. A breed of small yellow bird was developed from Gran Canaria birds, and these became known as canaries.

Canton Island is one of the many islands that make up the Palmyra Atoll. It was named for the New Bedford whaling ship *Canton*, which was shipwrecked there in March of 1854.

Captiva Island is located off the southwestern coast of Florida near Fort Myers, south of Port Charlotte and Gasparilla Island. It is believed to have been named by or for renowned pirate José Gaspar.

Gaspar made his headquarters at Port Charlotte, and he named Gasparilla Island for himself. Called the King of Pirates, he is said to have stolen as much as $30 million in booty. He is supposed to have killed all the men he captured and kept all the women. Captiva Island was given its name because of the women captives held there. In 1822, Gaspar attacked a U.S. gunboat disguised as a merchant ship. He was defeated, but before he could be captured, he wrapped himself in a heavy anchor chain and jumped overboard.

Carolines. This island archipelago in the Pacific Ocean was named for King Charles II of Spain (1661–1700).

Catalina Island is one of the Santa Barbara Islands, situated off the coast of California near Los Angeles. Originally called Santa Catalina Island, it was named in 1602 on the feast day of Saint Catherine of Alexandria by Spanish explorer Sebastian Vizcaíno (c. 1550–1616). *Catalina* is the Spanish form of Catherine.

Channel Islands. These are a group of British islands in the English Channel, so named because of their location. The three largest Channel Islands are Jersey, Guernsey, and Aldernay. They are famous for the fine breeds of cattle that bear their names.

Chappaquiddick Island. This island near Martha's Vineyard takes its name from the Wampanoag term meaning "place of separated island." In 1969, it was the scene of a famous automobile accident involving prominent politician Edward Kennedy.

Chichagof Island. This island lies just north of Baranof Island in the Alexander Archipelago of Alaska. It was named in 1805 for Admiral Vasili Yakov Chichagov of Russia who explored the area in 1765.

Cook Islands. Situated in the South Pacific, these islands were named for Captain James Cook

(1728–1779), who in 1773 was the first European to sight them.

East Indies. This term refers to the Malay Archipelago, Indonesia, and the Philippine Islands. Once called simply the Indies, they soon became confused with the West Indies, so they came to be called the East Indies to differentiate them.

Easter Island, located about twenty-four hundred miles from Chile, was given its name by Dutch Admiral Jakob Roggeveen, who first visited the island on Easter Sunday in 1722.

Falkland Islands. These islands were named for Viscount Falkland, British treasurer of the navy at the time John Strong first landed on them in 1690. Located about three hundred miles east of the Argentine coast, these islands were claimed by both Britain and Argentina until the British triumphed in a skirmish known as the Falklands War in 1982. The Argentine name for them is the Malvinas.

Florida Keys. This chain of coral islands and reefs along the southwest coast of Florida derives its name from the Spanish word *cayo*, which means "small island."

Formosa. The wild, forested beauty of this island led Portuguese traders in 1590 to name it *Formosa*, which is a Latin word meaning "beautiful." Taiwan is located on this island.

Galápagos Islands. Located six hundred miles west of Ecuador in the Pacific Ocean, this archipelago got its

name from *galápagos*, the Spanish word for "tortoises."
The giant tortoises on these islands sometimes weigh
more than three hundred pounds.

Gilbert Islands.   These sixteen low coral islands are
located in the central Pacific Ocean. They were named
for British navigator Captain James Gilbert, who explored them in 1788.

Greenland.   This is the largest island in the world. It
was optimistically named Greenland in order to attract
settlers. However, even during Greenland's short sum-
mers, only the southern coastal areas are green. Greenland is a territory of Denmark.

Ionian Islands.   These islands lie off the west coast of
Greece and Albania and form part of Greece. There
are seven large islands and many tiny islets in the
group. They were named the Ionian Islands after the
Greek nymph Io, who also gave her name to the Ionian
Sea.

Isle of Man.   This island in the Irish Sea, between Ireland and Britain, derives its name from the Celtic word
for "mountain." The people who live there are called
Manx.

Isle of Pines.   A Caribbean island belonging to Cuba,
it got its name from the fact that there are many pines
there. It is located about forty miles south of Cuba.

Iwo Jima   is the middle island of the three Volcano Islands in the northwestern Pacific Ocean. Its English
name is Sulphur Island, because sulphur was mined

there before World War II. *Iwo Jima* is Japanese for "sulphur island."

Leeward Islands. These islands in the West Indies were named Leeward because they were sheltered from the winds. *Leeward* is a sailing term that refers to the side of the ship that is protected from the wind.

Long Island, located south of New York, is 120 miles long and about 20 miles wide. The western end is occupied by Queens and Brooklyn, boroughs of New York City. It is one and one third larger than the area of Rhode Island and has a population greater than forty-three states. The descriptive name refers to its length and was first applied to it by Dutch explorers in the seventeenth century.

Louisiade Archipelago. This island group is part of Papua New Guinea, lying about one hundred miles southeast of the main island. They were named for French navigator Louis-Antoine de Bougainville (1729–1811), who explored the islands in 1768.

Mackinac Island. This island resort is located in Lake Huron between the two peninsulas of Michigan. Pronounced "mackinaw," its name derives from the Ojibway name *Michili-mackinak*, meaning "island of the large turtle." The island resembles a giant turtle resting in the water.

Madeira. This island group, located off the northwest coast of Africa, has a Portuguese name that means "heavily wooded" or "timber."

Marshall Islands. Located in the Pacific Ocean, these islands were visited by the Spanish in 1529, but they were named for the English captain Alexander Marshall, who explored them in 1788.

Martinique. This Caribbean island is a department of France. The name derives from the French spelling of Matigno, which was based on an original Carib name whose meaning is unknown.

Melanesia. This name applies to a large group of Pacific islands, including Bismarck, Fiji, New Caledonia, Santa Cruz, the Solomon Islands, and Vanuatu. The Greek name, which means "black islands," refers to the indigenous people, who have woolly hair and dark skin.

Micronesia. These islands stretch from east to west across twenty-seven hundred miles of the Pacific, and from north to south thirteen hundred miles. Although there are over two thousand islands in the group, only ninety-six are inhabited. Their Greek name means "tiny islands."

Montserrat is one of the islands of the West Indies. Columbus named it in 1493 after the Spanish mountain Montserrat.

Newfoundland Island is part of Newfoundland, one of the eastern provinces of Canada. In 1497, Italian explorer Giovanni Cabato (John Cabot, c. 1450–1499) was the first European to reach this island. He had been sent by King Henry VII of England in search of a western route to Asia, and since the shore he reached was obviously not the one he was seeking, it was referred to as "new-found land."

Padre Island, off the coast of Texas, is about one hundred miles long. It was named in honor of Father Nicolas Baille, a Spanish priest who owned a ranch there in about 1800. *Padre* is the Spanish word for "father."

Palmyra Atoll. This atoll, a ring-shaped group of fifty coral islets, is located about 960 miles south-southwest of Honolulu. The atoll was discovered in 1802 by the American ship *Palmyra*, and it was named the Atoll of Palmyra. It was originally claimed by Hawaii, but in 1912, the United States annexed it. Today it has an emergency landing strip for planes and is privately owned. *Palmyra*, meaning "palm city," is the name of an ancient Syrian city.

Pea Patch Island, in the Delaware River, got its name in an unusual way. It is said that a ship carrying a cargo of peas was wrecked on a sandbar where the island now stands. The peas sprouted and grew in the sand, catching more and more soil until an island was formed. It was thus given the appropriate name Pea Patch.

Polynesia is a group of Pacific islands that extends all the way from Hawaii to the north of New Zealand. The Greek name means "many islands."

Queen Charlotte Islands. These islands are in the North Pacific Ocean, about sixty miles off the coast of British Columbia. Captain George Dixon explored them in 1787 and named them for his ship, the *Queen Charlotte*.

Saint Vincent Island was, perhaps, named for the earl of Vincent, an English admiral who defeated the Spanish fleet under Don José de Cordoba in 1797.

Smith Island, named for New England pioneer Captain John Smith (c. 1580–1631), is Maryland's most remote island. It was named in 1608, one year after the founding of Jamestown, Virginia. The people of Smith Island live much as they did two hundred years ago. A ferry from Crisfield takes people to visit this charming old community, but no cars are allowed.

Solomon Islands. These were named in 1568 by Spanish navigator Alvaro de Mendaña de Nehra (1541–1595) after the biblical King Solomon, because he believed he had found the source of the gold used for Solomon's Temple in Jerusalem.

Spice Islands. These Indonesian islands were named for the many spices grown there, including nutmeg, cinnamon, cloves, pepper, and mace.

Tasmania is an island state of Australia. It was first named Van Diemen's Land, in honor of Anton Van Diemen, governor of the Netherlands Antilles, by Dutch explorer Abel Janszoon Tasman, who visited the island in 1842. In 1855, Great Britain acquired the island, and it was renamed in Tasman's honor.

Tierra del Fuego. The Spanish name means "land of fire," referring to the many campfires seen by Portuguese explorers. Tierra del Fuego is the southern tip of South America, separated from the continent by a narrow waterway called the Strait of Magellan. The border between Argentina and Chile runs through the center of Tierra del Fuego.

Vancouver Island, off the coast of British Columbia, was named for English captain George Vancouver (1757–1798), who sailed around it in 1792.

Virgin Islands. This name refers to two groups of small islands east of Puerto Rico. Columbus visited the Virgin Islands on his second voyage to the Americas in 1493. The charming beauty and untouched appearance of these hills rising from the sea fascinated him. He named the group of islands the Virgin Islands, in memory of Saint Ursula and her eleven thousand maidens.

Windward Islands. These are a group of islands that lie in the southeastern part of the West Indies. They stretch around the eastern end of the Caribbean Sea like stepping-stones to South America. The islands were given their name because they were exposed to the northeast trade winds. The Windward group includes Dominica, St. Lucia, St. Vincent and the Grenadines, and Grenada, all of whom became independent of Britain in the 1970s, and Martinique, a department of France.

West Indies. The West Indies are a long chain of islands that separate the Caribbean Sea from the Atlantic Ocean. The islands stretch in a two-thousand-mile curve from an area near the southern tip of Florida and the eastern tip of the Yucatan Peninsula in Mexico to the coast of Venezuela. The West Indies cover a land area of 91,125 square miles and have a population of more than 21 million. Cuba is the largest island. Sometimes the name Antilles is used for all these islands except the Bahamas.

When Columbus sailed west from Spain in 1492, he arrived among these islands. Believing he had reached India, he referred to them as the Indies. He died still believing they were the islands of India, and the islands continued to be called the Indies. Later, to distinguish them from the true islands of the Indies, they came to be called the West Indies.

Wrangel Island, a Russian possession in the Arctic Ocean off the coast of Siberia, was named for Russian explorer Admiral Baron Ferdinand Petrovich von Wrangel (1794–1870).

10

Mountains

Adirondack Mountains. These mountains were named for the Adirondack, an Algonquin group first recorded by Roger Williams (c. 1603–1683) as Mohawk. At one time, it is said, the Adirondack ate only fish and game, and chewed sassafras bark and tasty buds from the trees. The tribal name is believed to mean "leaf eaters."

Allegheny Mountains. Part of the Appalachians extending from Virginia to Pennsylvania, these mountains were named for the Allegheny River, which derives its name from the Leni-Lenapé term *welhik hanna*, "fine river," or *oolik hanna*, "beautiful river."

Alps. There are several possible origins for this ancient name. Some believe it derives from the Celtic word *alb*, meaning "white," being so named by the Gauls, or from the Latin *albus*, also meaning "white." The Swiss term *alp*, meaning "mountain pasture," may be the source, or perhaps the pre-Celtic Iberian word *alb*, meaning "height" or "hill." These high mountains in Switzerland are covered with snow most of the year, and the Alpine villages that dot their slopes draw tourists from around the world.

Andes Mountains. These mountains are much higher than either the Alps or the Rockies. Aconcagua, in Argentina near the border of Chile, is the highest peak in the Americas. It rises 22,835 feet above sea level. The Andes derive their name from either an old Inca word meaning "east," due to their point of view; or Anti, a tribal name; or the Peruvian word *anta*, meaning "copper;" or the Portuguese term *anta*, meaning "tapir."

Appalachian Mountains. This mountain range extends fifteen hundred miles from Newfoundland to Alabama and includes many different mountains: the Blue Ridge, the White, the Green, the Black, the Alleghenies, the Adirondacks, and the Great Smokies. The mountains were named for the Apalachee, a Native American branch of the Muskhogee. The name derives from the Choctaw word *apelachi*, meaning "helper."

Atlas Mountains. These mountains in present-day Morocco were named for Atlas, one of the mighty giants of Greek mythology. The early Greeks believed that the giants had warred against the gods and lost. All the giants were condemned to everlasting punishment for their sins. Atlas was to climb to the top of what are now the Atlas Mountains and forever hold up the sky to keep it from falling. The highest of the mountains ranges was then called Atlas, and finally all the mountains in the area came to have this name.

Bighorn Mountains. These Wyoming mountains, also spelled Big Horn, form the eastern front of the Rockies. They were named for the many bighorn sheep found in the area. The mountains are called *Ahsata* by the Native Americans, a name which means "bighorn."

Black Hills. These hills in South Dakota and part of northeastern Wyoming were named for the forests of blue-black pines that cover them. Their original Dakota name was *paha sapa*, "black hills."

Black Mountains. These mountains are part of the Pisgah National Forest in North Carolina. They were given their name because of the dark evergreen forests on their slopes. The Black Mountains include Mount Mitchell.

Blue Ridge Mountains. These form a range of the Appalachians, rising in West Virginia, Virginia, North and South Carolina, and part of Georgia. Their name refers to the bluish appearance of the pine-covered slopes as seen from a distance.

Cadillac Mountain. This mountain in Maine was named for Antoine de la Mothe Cadillac, the founder of Detroit, who was given a land grant here by the king of France.

Catskill Mountains. Part of the Appalachians in New York, they got their name from the Dutch phrase *Kats Kil*, meaning "cat's stream." It is not known for certain why this name was given to the area, but some believe it was derived from an earlier personal name. The name has given rise to many stories of giant wild cats being seen in the mountains.

Cumberland Mountains. Part of the Appalachians, separating Kentucky from Virginia and extending into

Tennessee, these mountains were named for William Augustus, duke of Cumberland (1721–1765), son of King George II of England.

Great Smoky Mountains. This range of the Appalachians, rising in Tennessee and North Carolina, was named for the haze, or smoky mist, which usually covers them.

Green Mountains. Part of the Appalachians in Vermont, these hills were named for dense evergreen forests that cover their slopes.

Himalayan Mountains. The highest mountain range in the world, the Himayalas were created by overlapping tectonic plates between Asia and India. *Himalaya* is a Sanskrit name which means "snow abode." Mount Everest is one of the Himalayan peaks.

K2. This is the official name of the second highest mountain in the world after Mount Everest. The name indicates that it was the second peak of the Karakoram range of the Himalayas to be surveyed. K2 was named in 1856 by Colonel T. G. Montgomery. Its unofficial name, Mount Godwin Austen, honors Henry Haversham Godwin Austen (1834–1933), an English surveyor who measured it in 1861. The peak rises 28,251 feet above sea level and was first successfully ascended in 1954.

La Sal Mountains. Located in Canyonlands National Park in Utah, these mountains are as white as the salt that inspired their name. *La sal* is Spanish for "the salt." Rising to an altitude of twelve thousand feet, they are a spectacular sight when covered with snow.

Matterhorn. This famous peak in the Swiss Alps derives its name from *matt*, "meadow," referring to pastureland at its base, coupled with the mountain's resemblance to a stag's horn.

Mauna Kea, a dormant volcano on the island of Hawaii, is the world's highest island peak, and often covered with snow. Its Hawaiian name means "white mountain."

Mauna Loa is the world's largest volcano. Its Hawaiian name means "long mountain."

Medicine Bow Range. This section of the Rocky Mountains, located in Colorado and Wyoming, was for many years the place Native Americans would collect wood for their bows, and also various ceremonial relics (known as "medicine"), thus giving the range its name.

Mont Blanc, the highest mountain in the Alps, derives its name from the French phrase *mont blanc*, meaning "white mountain."

Montserrat. This Spanish mountain's name literally means "mountain-serrated," referring to its jagged, rough appearance.

Mount Baker, in Washington, was named for Joseph Baker, an officer who accompanied explorer George Vancouver (1757–1798), who named it for him. Vancouver also named Puget Sound for one of his officers, and his own name has been given to several places on the Pacific northwest coast of North America.

Mount Chocorua. Many Native American legends are told in New Hampshire. One of these is the legend of

Chocorua, a Pequot who left his son to stay with white people while he was on a journey. The son was accidentally poisoned. For vengeance, Chorocua killed all the members of the family the boy had stayed with, and later he was killed on the slopes of the mountain that now bears his name. Before he died, he pronounced a curse on any white man who would live in the region. For years, cattle sickened and died in the region, and it was considered the result of the curse until a deadly natural chemical was found in the water. Chorocua is believed to be a Pennecook name derived from *tsikweres*, "frog."

Mount Cook, in New Zealand, was named for the English navigator James Cook (1728–1779), who was the first European to see it.

Mount Everest. High in the Himalayas on the border between India and China, this is the highest peak in the world. It was named for British surveyor Sir George Everest, who fixed the exact height of the peak in 1841.

Mount Fremont, in California, was named for explorer John C. Frémont (1813–1890), who climbed the 13,700-foot peak in 1842. There is also a Fremont Peak in Wyoming.

Mount Godwin Austen. See *K2*.

Mount of the Holy Cross. This mountain in west-central Colorado got its name in 1869 from the fact that there are two snow-filled crevasses on the mountain that form a huge cross near its peak.

Mount Hood, in Oregon, was named in 1792 by explorer George Vancouver (1757–1798) in honor of Lord Samuel Hood (1724–1816), a British admiral.

Mount Kilauea. This active volcano in Hawaii bears a Hawaiian name which means "spewing."

Mount Logan, the highest peak in Canada, was named for Sir William Edmond Logan, director of the Canadian Geological Survey.

Mount McKinley, in central Alaska, is the highest mountain in North America. It was named for William McKinley, the twenty-fifth U.S. president, who was assassinated in 1901.

Mount Mitchell, in the Black Mountains of North Carolina, was named for Dr. Elisha Mitchell (1793–1857), who fell to his death while attempting to measure its height. At 6,684 feet, it is the highest mountain east of the Mississippi.

Mount of Olives. One half mile east of Jerusalem, this mountain got its name from the olive trees that grow on it. According to the Bible, Jesus was on the Mount of Olives when he made his ascension into heaven.

Mount Olympus, in Washington State, was given this name by Captain James Meares in 1778. He named it for Mount Olympus in Greece because he felt that this mountain would also be a fine place for the gods to dwell.

Mount Rushmore, in South Dakota, was named for a New York attorney, Carlos E. Rushmore. One day when he was walking with a friend in the mountains, he asked the name of a certain peak and was told that it was Rushmore. The lawyer believed the joke, and he told friends about it when he returned to the boarding-house. The people who lived there thought it was a good joke and did not contradict him. He left thinking the peak was really called Rushmore. Those who were in on the joke continued to call it that until finally it actually did become known as Mount Rushmore. The giant carved figures of George Washington, Thomas Jefferson, Abraham Lincoln, and Theodore Roosevelt are located on the mountain.

Mount Tyndall, located in California, was named for British physicist and glacier scholar John Tyndall (1820–1893), who traveled and lectured in the American West.

Mount Wrangell. This peak in the Wrangell Mountains of Alaska was named for Russian explorer Admiral Baron Ferdinand Petrovich von Wrangel (1794–1870), when Russia held the territory. He also gave his name to Wrangel Island, which is still a Russian possession. The American spelling of his name, with two "l's," reportedly annoyed the admiral.

Ozark Mountains. Located in Missouri and Arkansas, and stretching into parts of Illinois and Oklahoma, they derive their name from the French phrase *aux arcs,* meaning "in the land of the Arkansas," referring to the Native American tribe that inhabited the area in the eighteenth century.

Pikes Peak is perhaps the best known of all the Rocky Mountain peaks in Colorado. It was named for explorer Lieutenant Zebulon Montgomery Pike (1779–1813), who in 1806 was the first European American to explore the mountain.

Rocky Mountains. This massive three-thousand-mile range, stretching from Mexico to Alaska, was given a simple, descriptive name.

Sierra Madre. This name is used for mountain ranges in Spain, Mexico, and the Luzon Islands of the Philippines. The Spanish name means "mother mountains."

Sugar Loaf Mountain. The conical shape of a colonial loaf of brown sugar, which resembled a mountain, inspired this popular name. Maine, New Hampshire, and Colorado have mountains with this name.

Tien Shan. This mountain range in central Asia, stretching across the border of Kirghizia to China, is the highest north of the Himalayas. Its Chinese name means "celestial mountains."

Unaka Mountains. Located in North Carolina and Tennessee, the Unakas derive their name from the Cherokee word meaning "white." The Unakas encompass the Great Smoky Mountains.

White Mountains. Part of the Appalachian Mountain system, these mountains stretch in a southeastern direction from Maine into New Hampshire. The White Mountains received their name because their rocky summits are often covered with snow.

Wichita Mountains. These Oklahoma mountains were named for the Wichita, a Caddo tribe whose name means simply "human being."

Recommended Reading

ABATE, FRANK R., editor. *American Places Dictionary: A Guide to 45,000 Populated Places, Natural Features, and Other Places in the United States.* Detroit: Omnigraphics, 1994.

ASOMIV, ISAAC. *Words on the Map.* Boston: Houghton Mifflin, 1962.

BLACKIE, C. *A Dictionary of Place Names, Giving Their Derivations.* 3d ed., revised. London: John Murray, 1887. Republished Detroit: Gale Research Company, 1968.

Central Intelligence Agency. *The World Fact Book.* Washington, D.C.: U.S. Government Printing Office, 1994.

EKWALL, EILERT. *The Concise Oxford Dictionary of English Place Names.* 4th ed. London: Oxford University Press, 1960, reprinted 1974.

PAXTON, JOHN. *The Statesman's Year-book World Gazetteer.* 4th ed. New York: St. Martin's Press, 1991.

SMITH, WHITNEY. *Flags Through the Ages and Across the World.* Maidenhead, England: McGraw-Hill, 1975.